2 Kings

An 11-Lesson Study Containing
Weekly Commentary
and
Daily Study Questions

by
Kathy Rowland

JOY OF LIVING
BIBLE STUDIES

Published by Joy of Living Bible Studies

For a free catalog please contact us at:

    800-999-2703 or 805-650-0838
    website: www.joyofliving.org
    e-mail: info@joyofliving.org

ISBN   1-932017-71-2
          978-1-932017-71-7

About Joy of Living

For over 45 years Joy of Living has been effectively establishing individuals around the world in the sound, basic study of God's Word.

Evangelical and interdenominational, Joy of Living reaches across denominational and cultural barriers, enriching lives through the simple, pure truths of God's inspired Word, the Bible.

Studies are flexible, suited for both formal and informal meetings, as well as for personal study. Each lesson contains historical background, commentary, and a week's worth of personal application questions, leading readers to discover fresh insights into God's Word. Courses covering many books in both the Old and New Testaments are available. Selected courses are also available in several foreign languages. Contact the Joy of Living office for details.

Joy of Living Bible Studies was founded by Doris W. Greig in 1971 and has grown to include classes in nearly every state in the Union and many foreign countries.

Table of Contents

How to Use Joy of Living Materials

This unique Bible study series may be used by people who know nothing about the Bible, as well as by more knowledgeable Christians. Each person is nurtured and discipled in God's Word, and many develop a personal relationship with Jesus Christ as they study.

Joy of Living is based on the idea that each person needs to open the Bible and let God speak to them by His Holy Spirit, applying the Scripture's message to their needs and opportunities, their family, church, job, community, and the world at large.

Only a Bible is needed for this study series. While commentaries may be helpful, it is not recommended that people consult them as they work through the daily study questions. It is most important to allow the Holy Spirit to lead them through the Bible passage and apply it to their hearts and lives. If desired, additional commentaries may be consulted after answering the questions on a particular passage.

The first lesson of a series includes an introduction to the study, plus the first week's daily study questions. Some questions are simple, and some are deeper for those who are more advanced. The individual works through the Bible passages each day, praying and asking God's guidance in applying the truth to their own life. (The next lesson will contain the commentary on the Bible passage being covered in the study questions.)

To Use in a Group Setting:

After the daily personal study of the passage has been completed, the class gathers in a small group, where they pray together and discuss what they have written in response to the questions about the passage, clarifying problem areas and getting more insight into the passage. The small group/discussion leader helps the group focus on biblical truth, and not just on personal problems. The student is the only person who sees their own answers and shares only what they feel comfortable sharing.

After small groups meet for discussion and prayer, they often gather in a large group meeting where a teacher gives a brief lecture covering the essential teaching of the Bible passage which was studied during the prior week and discussed in the small groups. The teacher may clarify the passage and challenge class members to live a more committed daily life.

At home, the student begins the next lesson, containing commentary notes on the prior week's passage and questions on a new Scripture passage.

Do You KNOW You Have Eternal Life?

Your Condition...
For all have sinned and fall short of the glory of God. (Romans 3:23)
But your iniquities (sins) have separated you from your God. (Isaiah 59:2)
For the wages of sin is death. (Romans 6:23)

There is help...
For Christ died for sins once for all, the righteous for the unrighteous, to bring you to God. (1 Peter 3:18)
The gift of God is eternal life in Christ Jesus our Lord. (Romans 6:23)

What do I do?...
Repent, then, and turn to God, so that your sins may be wiped out. (Acts 3:19)
Believe in the Lord Jesus, and you will be saved. (Acts 16:31)

You CAN know...
He who has the Son has life; he who does not have the Son of God does not have life. I write these things to you who believe in the name of the Son of God so that you may know that you have eternal life. (1 John 5:12-13)

If you would like to make the decision today to repent and trust Christ as your Savior, either for the first time or as a re-commitment of your life, you may want to pray a prayer similar to this one:

Lord Jesus, I admit that I am a sinner. Please forgive my sins. Thank You for dying on the cross for me, and for coming alive again. I accept Your gifts of forgiveness and eternal life. I place my life in Your hands. I want to be Yours forever. Thank you for loving me so much. In Your name I pray. Amen.

2 Kings
Lesson 1

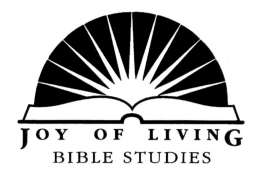

JOY OF LIVING
BIBLE STUDIES

God's Call, God's Promise
(Genesis 11-35)

Although the events in the books of 1 and 2 Kings took place from 930 BC to shortly after 561 BC,[1] the story really began nearly a thousand years earlier in the city of Ur of the Chaldees (in modern day Iraq). After God sent the flood that destroyed all life on earth except for the people and animals preserved on the ark, the descendants of Noah had spread out, multiplied and populated the earth, and they had again abandoned the God who created them.

Yet God had not abandoned humanity. He called one man, Abram, and told him that if he would leave his country and go to a land God would show him, He would give Abram that land, make a great nation from his descendants, and bless all the world through him. (It would be through his descendants that the Savior of the world would come.) In faith Abram (later called Abraham) obeyed God. Abraham had a son, Isaac, to whom the promise was given, and he in turn had a son, Jacob, to whom the promise was given.

From a Family to a Nation
(Genesis 46—Exodus 18)

Jacob, whose name God changed to Israel, had 12 sons. When Jacob was an old man, he, his sons, and their families (70 people in all) went into Egypt to escape starvation during a great famine. One of the sons, Joseph, was already there and in great power. He was second only to the Pharaoh, and because of this the family was well cared for.

However, generations passed, and the children of Israel grew in numbers. A new Pharaoh arose and was fearful of this great number of foreigners living within the borders of his land. To protect himself and his country, he placed the Israelites in bondage, where they remained for nearly 400 years. As always, God was faithful, and in His time He raised up a man named Moses. With great and mighty miracles God delivered the Israelites from the Egyptians and led them to the land He had promised to Abraham, Isaac, and Jacob.

A Covenant Made — A Covenant Broken
(Exodus 19 — Judges)

Prior to bringing the Israelites into the Promised Land, the general area of Israel today, God made a covenant with them. At Mount Sinai they agreed to serve the Lord and obey His commands. He gave them

His law, and promised to bless them as long as they served Him. But even as God gave them His glorious law, they were rebelling against Him and worshipping other gods. And so began the cycle of God's blessing, Israel's rebellion, God's disciplining, their repentance, God's deliverance and blessing again.

Because of their continued disobedience and rebellion, the Israelites wandered in the desert for 40 years after leaving Egypt and prior to entering the Promised Land. God, however, miraculously provided for them during that time. Finally, with Israel poised on the verge of entering the Promised Land, God designated Joshua, son of Nun, to lead them in the conquest of their new homeland. The final chapter of the book of Joshua states, "Israel served the Lord throughout the lifetime of Joshua and of the elders who outlived him and who had experienced everything the Lord had done for Israel" (Joshua 24:31).

The time of the judges began soon after the death of Joshua. Israel would again rebel against God and worship false gods. God would allow a nation to oppress them until they cried out to God in their misery. In mercy He would raise up a person to judge them and lead them in victory against their oppressor. As long as the judge lived, there was peace, but when the judge died, the Israelites soon slipped into their old ways. This was a time when "everyone did as they saw fit" (Judges 17:6)—and much of the time, anarchy reigned.

The Kingdom Established
1 Samuel 8 — 2 Samuel 24

Israel had been given the perfect government, with the Lord Himself as King, and the law of the Lord as the law of the land, yet the people weren't satisfied. They wanted to be like the nations round about them. They wanted a man as their king. God granted their desire.

Saul, their first king, didn't fully obey the Lord, so God gave the kingdom to David, a shepherd who loved the Lord. Although David made many mistakes, God said, "I have found David son of Jesse, a man after my own heart" (Acts 13:22).

The Kingdom's Exaltation and Exile
1 & 2 Kings

David could not live forever, and his son, Solomon, became king after him. Although God's hand of blessing was upon Solomon, and he achieved greatness for himself and the kingdom, his sin began the eventual decline and eventual division of the kingdom into the north-

1. Merrill C. Tenney, general editor. *The New International Dictionary of the Bible* (Grand Rapids: Zondervan, 1987).

ern kingdom of Israel and the southern kingdom of Judah. For the next several hundred years there was a pattern of disobedience and judgment, broken only by periodic revivals in the southern kingdom of Judah under the leadership of godly kings. This disobedience led to the deportation and exile of God's people from both kingdoms. Although humanity is unfaithful, God remains faithful to His promises. Hope was extended to God's people that they would eventually return to the land, and that one day the offspring of David would again sit on the throne—this time forever.

God's Plan

The Bible unfolds for us God's beautiful plan to redeem humanity and restore to us everything that was lost in the fall of Adam and Eve in the Garden of Eden. The conquest of the Promised Land and the consequent removal of the ungodly and wicked people living there were part of God's plan. His plan for Israel (see Romans 9:4-5) was…

- ✍ to establish a "holy nation" (Exodus 19:6).

- ✍ to give them His law and the temple worship.

- ✍ to reveal to them His glory.

- ✍ to bring forth through them the Messiah, the Savior, to redeem the world.

It was not that the Israelites were innately better than other nations. As the Bible plainly reveals, all of humanity is lost in sin (see Romans 3:23), and Israel repeatedly sinned. It is simply that God chooses to use whomever He will, and He chose to create and use the nation of Israel as part of His plan. Through them He would demonstrate to the world…

- ✍ that He alone is God.

- ✍ that He is completely holy.

- ✍ that all humanity is depraved.

- ✍ that sin is terrible.

- ✍ that we are helpless in our sin.

- ✍ that it is impossible to remove sin and its consequences by any natural means.

- ✍ that a Savior is necessary (see Galatians 3).

- ✍ that through them, finally, He would send His Son to be our Savior.

The Books of 1 and 2 Kings

First and Second Kings were originally one book, but the translators of the Septuagint, a pre-Christian Greek translation of the Old Testament, divided the book of Kings into two books because the Greek translation took up more space than the Hebrew version. These books are a sequel to 1 and 2 Samuel, and begin during the final days of King David's life. They cover approximately 400 years, and tell of Solomon's reign, of the division of the kingdom into the northern kingdom of Israel and the southern kingdom of Judah, and of the events leading to the downfall of these two kingdoms.

As you study 2 Kings (1 Kings is covered in a separate Joy of Living study), you will see the failure of God's people to obey Him, and the results of that disobedience. You will also see God's patience and His continued faithfulness and mercy to those who call upon His Name, even in the most evil of times.

Who Wrote 1 and 2 Kings?

There are varying opinions regarding what person or persons physically wrote 1 and 2 Kings. Jewish tradition holds that it was the prophet Jeremiah, although many contemporary scholars do not accept this. There are entire books written about who and when various portions of the Bible were written, and it is all very interesting and serves a purpose; however, our purpose in this study is to know God better, to understand His working on behalf of and through humanity.

And to that end, God solves for us the problem of "Who wrote 1 and 2 Kings?" He tells us simply that the Bible (including 1 and 2 Kings) is His Word, recorded by people but written by the Holy Spirit. Second Peter 1:21 says, "For prophecy never had its origin in the human will, but prophets, though human, spoke from God as they were carried along by the Holy Spirit." And 2 Timothy 3:16 says, "All Scripture is God-breathed…" Regardless of whom God used to record the Bible, He has spoken to us. The test of time has proven the infallibility of His Word.

Second Peter 1:19 says, "We also have the prophetic message as something completely reliable, and you will do well to pay attention to it, as to a light shining in a dark place…" As you work through the study of 2 Kings, ask God to open the eyes of your understanding to His truth. Ask Him to help you apply His truth to your own life.

A Daily Appointment with God

Make a daily appointment with God. Find a quiet spot. Take your Bible and your study material with you. If you have a busy phone, you may have to turn it off! Remember how very important your appointment with God is, and make time to be with Him daily. Ask yourself the following things:

1. How much time will I spend with the Lord each day?

2. What do I need to put aside in order to spend this time with the Lord? (Examples: sleep, TV, emailing, web-browsing or online chatting, casual telephone conversations, etc. Each person will have to decide what his or her priorities are, and what can be removed from the daily schedule to make time to spend with God.)

3. What is the best time for my appointment with God?

4. Where is the quietest place for me to pray and study?

5. Do I really want to spend time with God? (If your last answer is "yes," God will bless you as you work out the time. If your last answer is "no," pray that God will give you a desire, a hunger to spend this time with Him. He will do this for you!)

The Rulers of Israel and Judah

The United Kingdom of Israel and Judah

Saul	1050 - 1010 (40 years)
David	1010 - 970 (40 years)
Solomon	970 - 930 (40 years)

All dates are BC, and are based on *The NIV Study Bible*.[1]

The Southern Kingdom of Judah

Rehoboam	930 - 913 (17 years)
Abijah[2]	913 - 910 (3 years)
Asa*	910 - 869 (41 years)
Jehoshaphat*	872 - 869 (co-regent with Asa - 4 years)
	869 - 848 (sole reign - 21 years)
Jehoram	848 - 841 (8 years)
Ahaziah	841 (1 year)
Athaliah	841 - 835 (7 years)
Joash*	835 - 796 (40 years)
Amaziah	796 - 792 (5 years)
	792 - 782 (prisoner of Jehoash of Israel - 10 years)
	782 - 767 (released / overlap with Azariah - 14 years)
Azariah (Uzziah)	792 - 767 (overlap in reign with Amaziah - 24 years)
	767 - 740 (after Amaziah's death - 28 years)
Jotham	750 - 740 (co-regent with Azariah - 10 years)
	740 - 735 (sole reign - 6 years)
Ahaz	735 - 715 (16 years)
Hezekiah*	715 - 686 (29 years)
Manasseh	697 - 686 (co-regent with Hezekiah - 12 years)
	686 - 642 (sole reign - 43 years)
Amon	642 - 640 (2 years)
Josiah*	640 - 609 (31 years)
Jehoahaz	609 (3 months)
Jehoiakim	609 - 598 (11 years)
Jehoiachin	598 - 597 (3 months)
Zedekiah	597 - 586 (11 years)

Fall of the Southern Kingdom - 586

The Northern Kingdom of Israel

Jeroboam I	930 - 909 (22 years)
Nadab	909 - 908 (2 years)
Baasha	908 - 886 (24 years)
Elah	886 - 885 (2 years)
Zimri	885 (7 days)
Tibni	885 - 880 (ruled half of Israel - 6 years)
Omri	885 - 880 (ruled half of Israel - 6 years)
	880 - 874 (rulled all Israel - 6 years)
Ahab	874 - 853 (22 years)
Ahaziah	853 - 852 (2 years)
Joram	852 - 841 (12 years)
Jehu	841 - 814 (28 years)
Jehoahaz	814 - 798 (17 years)
Jehoash	798 - 782 (16 years)
Jeroboam II	793 - 782 (co-regent with Jehoash - 12 yrs)
	782 - 753 (sole reign - 29 years)
Zechariah	753 (6 months)
Shallum	752 (1 month)
Menahem	752 - 742 (ruled in Samaria - 10 years)
Pekahiah	742 - 740 (ruled in Samaria - 2 years)
Pekah	752 - 740 (ruled in Gilead - 12 years)
	740 - 732 (ruled over all Israel - 8 years)
Hoshea	732 - 722 (9 years)

Fall of the Northern Kingdom - 722

*In Judah, the southern kingdom, there were a few godly rulers among many who were evil. These godly rulers are marked with an asterik. In Israel, the northern kingdom, there were no godly rulers at all, but a continual succession of rulers who walked in idolatrous ways.

1. Kenneth Barker, editor. *The NIV Study Bible* (Grand Rapids: Zondervan, 1985). See charts: "Old & New Testament Chronology," "Rulers of Israel and Judah." The number of years listed in parentheses may appear incorrect when calculated from the dates, but most are taken directly from the NIV chart; others are estimated based on co-reigns, overlaps, etc.
2. This king is called "Abijam" in many other Bible versions.

Where 2 Kings Took Place

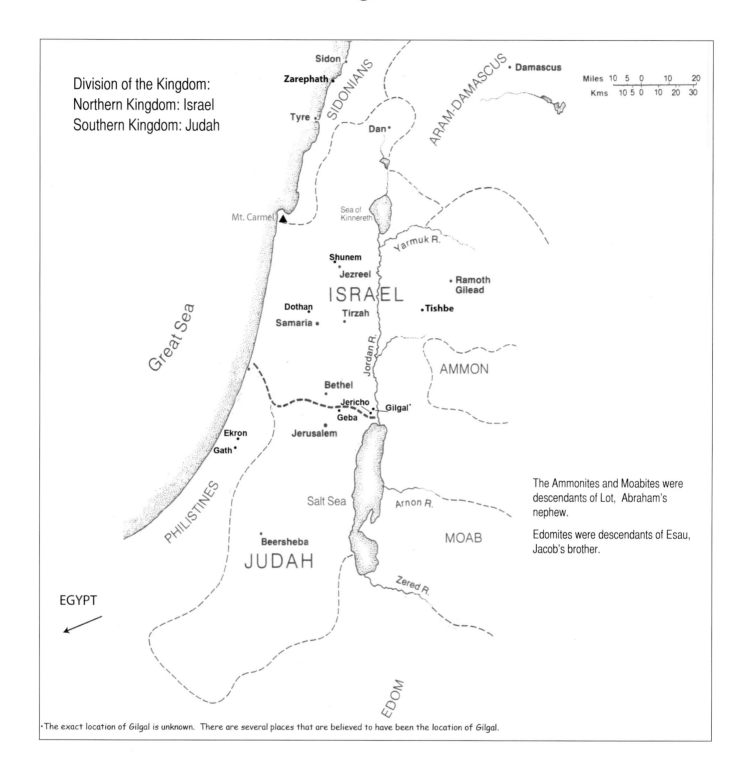

Division of the Kingdom:
Northern Kingdom: Israel
Southern Kingdom: Judah

The Ammonites and Moabites were descendants of Lot, Abraham's nephew.

Edomites were descendants of Esau, Jacob's brother.

•The exact location of Gilgal is unknown. There are several places that are believed to have been the location of Gilgal.

Adapted from *Reproducible Maps, Charts, TimeLines & Illustrations* (Ventura: Gospel Light. 1989). Used by permission. Some locations are approximate.

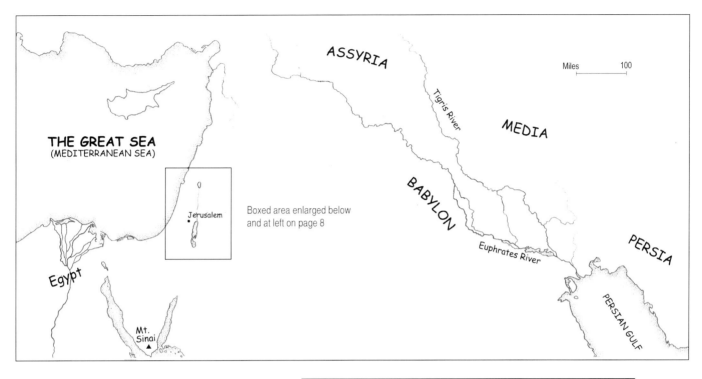

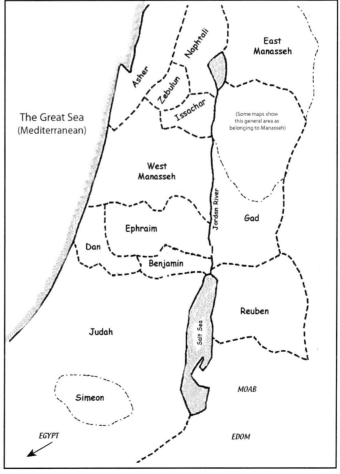

Distribution of the Land Among the Tribes of Israel

Adapted from *Reproducible Maps, Charts, TimeLines & Illustrations* (Ventura: Gospel Light. 1989). Used by permission. Some locations are approximate.

Study Questions

Before you begin your study this week:
- ਟੋ Pray and ask God to speak to you through His Holy Spirit.
- ਟੋ Use only the Bible for your answers.
- ਟੋ Write down your answers and the verses you used.
- ਟੋ Answer the "Challenge" questions if you have the time and want to do them.
- ਟੋ Share your answers to the "Personal" questions with the class only if you want to share them.

First Day: Read the Introduction to 2 Kings.

1. What meaningful or new thought did you find in the Introduction to 2 Kings or from your teacher's lecture?

2. Look for a verse in the lesson to memorize this week. Write it down, carry it with you, or post it in a prominent place. Make a real effort to learn the verse and its "address" (reference of where it is found in the Bible).

Second Day: Read 2 Kings 1-2, concentrating on 2 Kings 1.

1. King Ahaziah of Israel was introduced to us at the end of 1 Kings. Read 1 Kings 22:51-53 and describe his reign and his character.

2. a. After Ahaziah was seriously injured in a fall, what god did he consult? (2 Kings 1:2)

   b. How did God deal with Ahaziah's action? (2 Kings 1:3-4)

3. When Ahaziah found out that God had sent Elijah to meet his messengers and heard God's rebuke and judgment, what did he do? (2 Kings 1:5-9, summarize briefly)

4. a. With what attitude did the first two captains and their men approach Elijah, and what was the result? (2 Kings 1:9b-12)

b. How did the third captain and his men approach Elijah, and what happened this time? (2 Kings 1:13-15)

5. a. What was Ahaziah's fate because of his stubborn disbelief and continued wickedness? (2 Kings 1:16-17a)

b. Read 2 Kings 1:17b and 3:1. Who succeeded Ahaziah as king of Israel?[1]

6. Personal: Ahaziah thought only he and his messengers knew of his mission to consult Baal-Zebub, the god of Ekron. It must have been a shock to hear that God had sent Elijah to intercept his messengers and deliver a sentence of death. Yet Ahaziah continued in his stubborn rebellion and refused to repent. God sent His Son, Jesus Christ, not only to confront us with our sinfulness, but also to make it possible for us to be forgiven our sins and made right with God (see John 3:16-18). Have you listened to God's message, repented, and asked for forgiveness through Jesus Christ? If not, why not do it now? (See page 4 for more information.)

Third Day: Review 2 Kings 1-2, concentrating on 2 Kings 2:1-12.

1. a. Who was traveling with Elijah as his ministry on earth neared its end? (2 Kings 2:1)

b. Challenge: Read and briefly summarize 1 Kings 19:14-21. What were Elijah's circumstances when God directed him to call Elisha as his successor?

2. What miracle did God work through Elijah at the Jordan River? (2 Kings 2:8)

3. a. How did Elijah show his concern for his successor, Elisha? (2 Kings 2:9a)

---

1. The NIV calls this king of Israel Joram (the son of Ahab and brother of Ahaziah), but other Bible versions call him Jehoram, which is a variant of the name Joram. During part of Joram's reign over Israel, Jehoram son of Jehoshaphat ruled in Judah, first as co-regent with his father Jehoshaphat, and later as sole ruler. To avoid confusion, we will follow NIV usage and call the king of Israel Joram and the king of Judah Jehoram.

b. What did Elisha ask for? (2 Kings 2:9b)

c. Only God could grant this request. How would Elisha know whether God had done so? (2 Kings 2:10)

4. How did God take Elijah to heaven? (2 Kings 2:11)

5. How did Elisha show his grief at the loss of his mentor? (2 Kings 2:12)

6. Personal: Do you have a spiritual father or mother, a person who has mentored you in the faith? Are you grateful for the spiritual guidance you have received from them? Have they gone to be with the Lord in heaven already? If so, how did you feel? If they are still living, why not write them a note or call them, and tell them how much they have meant to you?

Fourth Day: Review 2 Kings 1-2, concentrating on 2 Kings 2:13-18.

1. a. Elisha had seen Elijah taken from him by the Lord's chariot and horses of fire, confirming that Elijah's spiritual power would continue in him (see 2 Kings 2:9-12). What further sign of this transfer did he find that Elijah had left behind? (2 Kings 2:13)

    b. Challenge: Review 1 Kings 19:16-19. How had Elijah signified that Elisha was to succeed him as prophet? What meaning did this give to the item Elijah left behind in 2 Kings 2:13?

2. What happened when Elisha called upon the Lord and repeated Elijah's actions beside the Jordan River? (2 Kings 2:14)

3. What did this miracle confirm to the fifty prophets from Jericho that were watching, and how did they act toward Elisha? (2 Kings 2:15)

4. a. What did the group of prophets have difficulty understanding, and what did they insist on doing because of this? (2 Kings 2:16-17a)

    b. Review 2 Kings 2:11. Where had the Spirit of the Lord actually taken Elijah?

5. What was the result of the prophets' search? (2 Kings 2:17b-18)

6. Personal: Elisha was an ordinary farmer that God called to be Elijah's successor. He knew that he did not have spiritual power in himself to follow in Elijah's footsteps, and God graciously granted his request for spiritual power. Unlike Old Testament believers, upon whom the Spirit came only for special purposes, every person who believes in Jesus Christ for salvation receives the gift of the Holy Spirit (see Titus 3:4-6). Have you thanked God for this gift? Do you depend upon the Holy Spirit to guide and empower you?

Fifth Day: Review 2 Kings 1-2, concentrating on 2 Kings 2:19-22.

1. Review 2 Kings 2:18 to see where Elisha was staying.

2. What problem did the people of this city bring to Elisha? (2 Kings 2:19)

3. We are not told why the water of Jericho was bad. How did Elisha, by the power of the Lord, help them? (2 Kings 2:20-22)

4. Personal: God delights in using ordinary things.[1] In Exodus 15:23-25 God instructed Moses to throw a piece of wood into bitter water in order to make it sweet. Here God instructs Elisha to throw a bowl full of salt into the water so it would no longer cause death. There was nothing "scientific" or "magical" about the salt. God spoke, Elisha obeyed, and God—not the salt—healed the water. First Corinthians 1:26-29 says, "Brothers and sisters, think of what you were when you were called. Not many of you were wise by human standards; not many were influential; not many were of noble birth. But God chose the foolish things of the world to shame the wise; God chose the weak things of the world to shame the strong. God chose the lowly things of this world and the despised things—and the things that are not—to nullify the things that are, so that no one may boast before him." Do you sometimes feel that you are too ordinary for God to use you? Remember, Elisha obeyed God; then God did the work—and God received the glory. Are you willing to obey God? Underline verse 29 in the above quotation from 1 Corinthians. How does this encourage you?

Sixth Day: Review 2 Kings 1-2, concentrating on 2 Kings 2:23-25.

1. a. Where did Elisha go next? (2 Kings 2:23a)

   b. Challenge: Read 1 Kings 12:26-33. What had Jeroboam, the first king of the northern kingdom of Israel, set up in Bethel less than 100 years earlier? From this, what do you think might have been the spiritual atmosphere in Bethel when Elisha went there?

---

1. A few of the ordinary things God has used are Moses' staff (see Exodus 4 for the first instance), the jawbone of a donkey in the hand of Samson (see Judges 15:15), and the trumpets, torches, and empty jars in the hands of Gideon and his men (see Judges 7:15ff).

2. In Jericho, the people had come to Elisha for help and followed his instructions in order that God would heal their water. What happened, in contrast, when he went to Bethel? (2 Kings 2:23)

3. a. The jeering remarks to Elisha were ultimately aimed at the God whom he represented. How did Elisha deal with this threat to his prophetic ministry? (2 Kings 2:24) What did God cause to happen?

   b. What do you learn about a curse from Proverbs 26:2?

4. a. From the number of boys involved, we see that this was not just a couple of youths making foolish comments, but a whole gang of youthful ruffians who viewed the Lord and His representative with contempt. This may seem an excessive sentence[1] that God carried out upon these unbelievers. However, God acted to validate and preserve the authority of Elisha's prophetic ministry, which would be to the entire northern kingdom of Israel. What do you learn from Romans 3:23 and 6:23a about the sentence that every person deserves?

   b. From Romans 6:23b, what provision has God made so that a person may escape this sentence?[2]

5. The NET Bible Notes explain, "The two brief episodes recorded in [2 Kings 2:] vv. 19-25 demonstrate Elisha's authority and prove that he was the legitimate prophetic heir of Elijah. He has the capacity to bring life and blessing to those who recognize his authority [is from God], or death and judgment to those who reject him [thus rejecting God and His messenger]."[3] What did Elisha do after this last incident? (2 Kings 2:25)

6. Personal: It is good for us to be reminded of the sentence that hangs over the head of every person who has not put their faith in Jesus Christ. Whom do you know that needs to hear about Jesus' gift of living water? Write down what you will tell them here. Pray that God will give you the opportunity and the right words at the right time to share His message with this person.

---

1. This does not necessarily mean that they were killed. According to Merriam Webster's Online Dictionary, "maul" means: "to attack and injure [someone] in a way that cuts or tears skin: to attack [someone] and cause a bloody injury."
2. To learn more about this, speak with your pastor, leader, or some other knowledgeable Christian. Or, you may turn to page 4.
3. *New English Translation/NET Bible Notes*. NET Bible® copyright ©1996-2016 by Biblical Studies Press, L.L.C. (http://netbible.com).

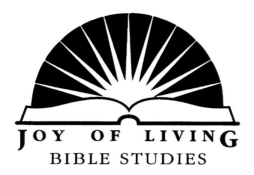

2 Kings
Lesson 2

JOY OF LIVING
BIBLE STUDIES

2 Kings Chapters 1-2

Setting: The Northern Kingdom of Israel

As 2 Kings opens, Elijah the Tishbite was serving as God's prophet to the northern kingdom of Israel. Elijah was first introduced to us and to Israel in 1 Kings 17. God had sent Elijah to stand against the worship of Baal during the reign of Ahab. He had been given power to shut up the heavens, so there was no rain for three and a half years. At the close of that time, he called down fire from heaven before the prophets of Baal at Mount Carmel. Ahab called him "you troubler of Israel" (1 Kings 18:17), refusing to admit that it was his own wickedness that had caused Israel's troubles.

Ahab died at the end of 1 Kings. Continuing the long line of wicked kings in the northern kingdom of Israel, Ahaziah had succeeded his father Ahab as king. We first met Ahaziah at the end of 1 Kings: "He did evil in the eyes of the Lord, because he followed the ways of his father and mother and of Jeroboam son of Nebat, who caused Israel to sin. He served and worshiped Baal and aroused the anger of the Lord, the God of Israel, just as his father had done" (1 Kings 22:52-53).

The Consequences of Sin

The Lord's anger against Ahaziah, as he continued in his father Ahab's wickedness, resulted in several forms of negative consequences:

- ❧ Political: "After the death of Ahab, Moab rebelled against Israel" (2 Kings 1:1). Much earlier, King David had conquered Moab, an area east of the Jordan River. After the northern kingdom of Israel broke away from the southern kingdom of Judah, Israel apparently continued the domination of Moab. Now Moab saw its chance and broke free of subjugation to Israel.

- ❧ Economic: Ahaziah joined with King Jehoshaphat of Judah in building ships to go to Tarshish. A prophet of the Lord told Jehoshaphat that because of his alliance with the wicked northern king, the Lord would destroy the ships—"And the ships were wrecked" (2 Chronicles 20:37; see also 1 Kings 22:48-49).

- ❧ Personal: Ahaziah fell "through the lattice of his upper room in Samaria" (2 Kings 1:2) and severely injured himself.

This injury provided an opportunity to see where Ahaziah would turn in a crisis. Rather than call on the Lord God of Israel, Ahaziah sent messengers to consult Baal-Zebub, the god of the Philistine city of Ekron, to see if he would recover from his injury.

The angel of the Lord told the prophet Elijah the Tishbite,[1] "Go up and meet the messengers of the king of Samaria and ask them, 'Is it because there is no God in Israel that you are going off to consult Baal-Zebub, the god of Ekron?' Therefore this is what the Lord says: 'You will not leave the bed you are lying on. You will certainly die!'" (2 Kings 1:3-4).

Whether Ahaziah had previous experience with Elijah we aren't told. But his father Ahab's experiences with the prophet were well known. Since Ahaziah also refused to obey the Lord, he would not have considered consulting Elijah about his injury.

Where we initially turn in times of crisis reveals whom or what we are trusting in. When a little child falls down and gets hurts they usually run to their mother, or to whomever is their main caregiver—the person they rely on to take care of them. When crisis strikes, where do you turn? Is your first reaction to call on the Lord for help, even while you are taking necessary action? Our reactions tell a lot about what is in our heart.

When Ahaziah's messengers returned to him, they said "a man" had sent him a message. After hearing the message and a description of the man—he wore a garment of hair (probably sheepskin or camel hair) and a leather belt around his waist—Ahaziah knew it had to be Elijah. He sent a captain with his company of 50 men to summon Elijah. The captain said to Elijah, who was sitting on the top of a hill, "Man of God, the king says, 'Come down!'" (2 Kings 1:9). To this peremptory, arrogant challenge, Elijah answered, "If I am a man of God, may fire come down from heaven and consume you and your fifty men!"—and it did! The king and his captains didn't learn quickly. Ahaziah sent a second delegation with the same message, and with the same terrifying result.

Because God is patient and longsuffering, and His judgment isn't usually immediate, people—even His own people—tend to forget to show Him the honor and respect that is due to Him. For example, consider how often the Lord's name is taken in vain. It is not uncommon

---

1. The Lord usually spoke directly to the consciousness of the prophet. The means of revelation may have been changed in this instance as a contrast between the messengers of Ahaziah and the "angel" (which means "messenger") of the Lord. [*NIV Study Notes* on 2 Kings 1:3]

to hear even young children say, "Oh, my ___." Matthew 12:34-36 tells us that what is in our heart is revealed by what comes out of our mouth, and that we will be held accountable for everything we say—since it is merely a reflection of who we really are. Pay attention to the words that flow from your mouth. What do they say about your heart?

Now the third captain followed orders and came to Elijah; however, he came humbly, begging for his life and the lives of his men. His attitude showed respect and fear of God's prophet (and therefore of God). His life and the lives of his men were spared. God is merciful.

The angel of the Lord told Elijah to go with him to see the king, and promised him safety. Elijah went to Ahaziah and repeated the Lord's message to him. And Ahaziah died, just as Elijah had prophesied. The word of the Lord was proved reliable and unconquerable.

Because Ahaziah didn't have a son, his brother Joram[1] succeeded him as king of Israel.

Elijah Taken up to Heaven

In 1 Kings 19:16, God had instructed Elijah to anoint Elisha son of Shaphat to be the one who would eventually succeed him as prophet. Elijah obeyed, and Elisha became a follower of and a servant to Elijah.

Although Israel, as a whole, no longer worshipped and served the Lord, God had told Elijah, "I reserve seven thousand in Israel—all whose knees have not bowed down to Baal and whose mouths have not kissed him" (1 Kings 19:18). Among these were members of groups referred to as "the company of the prophets"[2] or sometimes just as "the prophets." They generally lived together at religious training centers. Their chief study was the law and its interpretation. They were not necessarily prophets as we think of them—speaking messages from God—but they denounced national, family, and personal sin (see 1 Kings 20:35-42; 2 Kings 17:13). Years prior to this time, the first of these groups had been formed by Samuel in Ramah (see 1 Samuel 19:19-20). Now, in 2 Kings, these schools were flourishing at Bethel, Jericho, Gilgal, and elsewhere (see 2 Kings 2:3,5; 4:38; 6:1).

In 2 Kings chapter 2, Elijah and Elisha traveled together from Gilgal toward Bethel and then on to Jericho. It appears that Elijah was visiting, and possibly encouraging, the men who resided at these religious communities one final time.[3] Elijah urged Elisha to remain with each group they visited, but Elisha was determined to stay with his master. In both Bethel and Jericho, members of the company of the prophets asked Elisha about Elijah's imminent departure, but Elisha refused to speak of it. When Elijah and Elisha left for the Jordan, 50 of the company of the prophets at Jericho followed, waiting to see what the Lord would do. At the edge of the river, they witnessed a miracle—Elijah rolled up his cloak and used it to strike the river. Then, just as God had done for Moses at the Red Sea (see Exodus 14:21) and for the Israelites as they crossed the Jordan when they entered

the Promised Land (see Joshua 3:15-16), the waters divided. Elijah and Elisha then crossed over on dry ground.

Knowing that this would be his last day on earth, Elijah asked his servant what he could do for him. Elisha asked to "inherit a double portion of your spirit" (2 Kings 2:9). This request referred to Israelite inheritance laws that assigned a double portion of a father's possessions to the firstborn son (see Deuteronomy 21:17). That son then carried the responsibility of being the head of that family. And so, Elisha wasn't asking for a ministry twice as great as Elijah's. Rather, he was asking for spiritual power far beyond his own capabilities, in order to carry out the responsibilities of succeeding Elijah's ministry.[4]

Elijah's reply, "You have asked a difficult thing," meant that it was not in his own power to grant Elisha's request. He left the answer to the request in the Lord's hands, saying, "If you see me when I am taken from you, it will be yours—otherwise, it will not" (2 Kings 2:10).

Suddenly, as the two prophets continued on their journey, "a chariot of fire and horses of fire appeared and separated the two of them, and Elijah went up to heaven in a whirlwind." The *NIV Study Notes* say, "The Lord's heavenly host has accompanied and supported Elijah's ministry...and now at his departure Elisha is allowed to see it."[5]

When Elisha saw how Elijah was taken into heaven, he cried out, "My father! My father! The chariots and horsemen of Israel!" (2 Kings 2:12). Elijah, rather than the wicked king of Israel, had been the Lord's representative, the true strength of the nation of Israel.[6] The same words were later used of Elisha, as he lay dying, in 2 Kings 13:14.

What a great reminder to us that God and His angels are always present and working on behalf of His people (see Psalm 34:7). Elijah and Elisha lived before the death and resurrection of Jesus and the outpouring of the Holy Spirit. In this passage in 2 Kings, Elisha is encouraged by seeing just a bit of God's power. We, however, live on the resurrection side of the cross and have the Holy Spirit actually living within us. In 2 Corinthians 5:7 we are told, "We live by faith, not by sight." God is continually proving to us through His Word and through what He does in our lives that He is always present and working on our behalf.

Elijah did not experience death—he was taken bodily to heaven, into the presence of God.[7] This had happened once before in Scripture. In Genesis 5:24 we read, "Enoch walked faithfully with God; then he was no more, because God took him away." Enoch was "com-

---

1. Some Bible versions call him "Jehoram." See footnote on page 11.
2. In Hebrew they are referred to as "sons of the prophets." (*NET Bible Notes* on 2 Kings 2:3)
3. *NIV Study Bible Notes* on 2 Kings 2:3.

4. There are various opinions among Bible commentators about what a "double portion of your spirit" means.
5. *NIV Study Notes* on 2 Kings 2:11. In 2 Kings 6:17 Elisha will encourage his frightened servant by asking God to open the servant's eyes to see, "the hills full of horses and chariots of fire all around Elisha."
6. Ibid, notes on 2 Kings 2:12.
7. Elijah had not, at this point, finished his work for God. In the New Testament, he and Moses appear with Jesus when Jesus is transfigured (see Matthew 17:3, Mark 9:4, Luke 9:30). Many believe he is one of the two witnesses in Revelation 11:3—for a period of 1,260 days, God's two witnesses will testify of God before a world that has sold its allegiance to Satan and Satan's Antichrist.

mended as one who pleased God" in Hebrews 11:5, and we see from Elijah's ministry that he, too, pleased God.

Elijah's life had been one of service to the Lord. Elijah stood for the Lord and spoke His Word before a nation that, as a whole, had turned from God and sold its allegiance to other gods and the wicked practices that accompanied their worship.

We, as God's people, have been called to speak His truth to those around us. The same Spirit that empowered Elijah—the Holy Spirit—lives in us and empowers us to share His truth (see Acts 1:8). Ask Him to give you the boldness to tell others of His salvation. If you don't, who will?

Elisha Assumes Elijah's Ministry

Elijah's cloak had fallen from him as he was whirled away in the chariot of fire. When Elijah had first called Elisha to succeed him as prophet, Elijah went up to him and threw his cloak around him (see 1 Kings 19:19), so this cloak had tremendous meaning to Elisha. He now picked up the cloak and went back to the bank of the Jordan River. Just as Elijah had done, Elisha struck the water with the cloak, and once again the river parted. This confirmed Elisha's succession to Elijah's ministry, both to himself and to the fifty from the company of the prophets who had witnessed the entire event.

The prophets insisted on sending men to search for Elijah, in case "the Spirit of the Lord has picked him up and set him down on some mountain or in some valley" (2 Kings 2:16). Elisha finally gave in to their desire. Of course, they did not find Elijah, as they finally reported to Elisha. He couldn't resist saying, "Didn't I tell you not to go?"

Elisha's Miracles

Elisha's ministry opened with miracles that established the character of his ministry. His would be a helping ministry to those in need, but also would allow no disrespect for God and His earthly representatives.[1]

Elisha was staying in Jericho when the men from the company of the prophets were searching for Elijah. The people of the city asked for his help, because their water was bad and their land was unproductive.

Elisha asked the people to bring him a new bowl with salt in it, which he threw into the spring, saying, "This is what the Lord says: 'I have healed this water. Never again will it cause death or make the land unproductive'" (2 Kings 2:21). The salt was not magic—the Lord Himself healed, or purified, the water.

We may pray that a person is healed, and then they are, but we did not heal that person—God did. We may pray for a need, and it may be miraculously met, but we aren't the ones who met the need—God did. We must always remember that God does the miracles.

Next, Elisha went to Bethel. King Jeroboam of Israel had established this city as one of two religious centers for his kingdom, as he feared the people would return their allegiance to the king of Judah if they went to the temple in Jerusalem to worship. He made two golden calves and set them up in Bethel and in Dan, telling the people, "It is too much for you to go up to Jerusalem. Here are your gods, Israel, who brought you up out of Egypt" (1 Kings 12:28).

In contrast to Elisha's experience in Jericho, where the people came to Elisha for help and followed his instructions by faith, he ran into quite a different type of attention in Bethel: "As he was walking along the road, some boys came out of the town and jeered at him. 'Get out of here, baldy!' they said. 'Get out of here, baldy!'" (2 Kings 2:23). These boys not only insulted Elisha himself but also the God whom he represented. Elisha called down a curse on them in the name of the Lord, upon which two bears came out of the woods and mauled forty-two of the boys. From the number of boys involved, we see that this was not just a couple of youths making stupid comments, but a whole gang of ruffians who viewed the Lord and His representative with contempt.

Covenant Blessings and Curses

Elisha's first miracle illustrated God's covenant blessings that would come to all those who looked to Him for help. His second miracle, following the pronouncement of a curse, gave a warning to all of the northern kingdom of Israel of the judgment that would fall on them if they continued in their disobedience and apostasy. Second Chronicles 36:15-16 describes God's continual efforts to reach His people: "The Lord, the God of their ancestors, sent word to them through his messengers again and again, because he had pity on his people and on his dwelling place. But they mocked God's messengers, despised his words and scoffed at his prophets until the wrath of the Lord was aroused against his people and there was no remedy." God's covenant curses would fall on those who turned away from Him.

Jesus came and established a new covenant with humanity by dying on the cross and shedding His blood for our sin. Those who look to Him for salvation receive God's covenant blessing, resulting in new and eternal life in Christ. But those who turn away from God and from His Son Jesus, will experience His covenant curse—eternal separation from Him, in "the eternal fire prepared for the devil and his angels" (Matthew 25:41).

Have you accepted Jesus' gift of salvation? (If you need more information, turn to page 4.) Whom do you know who may still be living under the curse of death? Pray that God will give you the opportunity and the right words at the right time to share His message with them. Jesus said, "Very truly I tell you, whoever hears my word and believes him who sent me has eternal life and will not be judged but has crossed over from death to life" (John 5:24).

---

1. Frank E. Gaebelein, editor. *The Expositor's Bible Commentary* (Grand Rapids: Zondervan, 1990), notes on 2 Kings 2:19-22.

Study Questions

Before you begin your study this week:

- Pray and ask God to speak to you through His Holy Spirit.
- Use only the Bible for your answers.
- Write down your answers and the verses you used.
- Answer the "Challenge" questions if you have the time and want to do them.
- Share your answers to the "Personal" questions with the class only if you want to share them.

First Day: Read the Commentary on 2 Kings 2.

1. What meaningful or new thought did you find in the Commentary on 2 Kings 2 or from your teacher's lecture?

2. Look for a verse in the lesson to memorize this week. Write it down, carry it with you, or post it in a prominent place. Make a real effort to learn the verse and its "address" (reference of where it is found in the Bible).

Second Day: Read 2 Kings 3-4, concentrating on 3:1-14.

1. a. What was the spiritual evaluation of the reign of Joram son of Ahab?[1] (2 Kings 3:1-2a)

   b. What positive action did Joram take? (2 Kings 3:2b)

   c. How did he continue to lead Israel in apostasy? (2 Kings 3:3; review 1 Kings 12:26-33 for specific information on Jeroboam's sin)

2. a. When Moab rebelled against Israel, what did Joram do? (2 Kings 3:4-7a)

   b. When Jehoshaphat agreed to help Israel fight Moab, what route did he suggest, and what additional king joined them? (2 Kings 3:7b-9a)

3. a. What problem did the three allied armies run into? (2 Kings 3:9b)

   b. How did Joram and Jehoshaphat react very differently to this situation? (2 Kings 3:10-12)

4. a. How did Elisha rebuke Joram? (2 Kings 3:13a)

---

1. Some Bible versions call him "Jehoram." See footnote on page 11.

b. How did Joram respond? (2 Kings 3:13b)

5. What was the only reason Elisha was willing to help the allies? (2 Kings 3:14)

6. Personal: Joram may have felt that he was pretty good, since he got rid of the sacred stone of Baal that his father had made, and that therefore the Lord should look with favor on him. Yet he still "clung to the sins of Jeroboam" (2 Kings 3:3), continuing to worship the two golden calves set up at Bethel and Dan, and maintaining the false prophets attached to that worship. Elisha's rebuke stripped away any pretense Joram may have held about his status in the Lord's eyes. Is there anything in your life that you are trusting in more than you trust in God? Perhaps you have turned away from trust in one thing, but something else remains that still keeps you from truly trusting in God alone. Why not pray about this now?

Third Day: Review 2 Kings 3-4, concentrating on 3:15-27.

1. What did the Lord reveal to the kings through Elisha? (2 Kings 3:15-19)

2. How was Elisha's prophecy fulfilled? Compare the following passages.

   2 Kings 3:17 with 3:20

   2 Kings 3:18b-19 with 3:21-25

3. How did the king of Moab attempt to escape total defeat? (2 Kings 3:26-27a)

4. a. Challenge: The sacrifice of a child illustrates the terrible consequences that follow when people turn away from the revelation of the one true God and worship false gods. How does the apostle Paul describe this process in Romans 1:18-23?

   b. Challenge: We are horrified at the thought of child sacrifice, but there are many other behaviors that are also consequences of turning away from God. What else does Paul list in Romans 1:28-31?

5. Personal: What consequences of turning away from God have you seen in your own life (perhaps in the past), or in the lives of people around you?

Fourth Day: Review 2 Kings 3-4, concentrating on 4:1-7.

1. Who came to Elisha, and what crisis did she face? (2 Kings 4:1)

2. Challenge: Read Exodus 21:2-4; Leviticus 25:39-41; and Deuteronomy 15:1-11. Although not the ideal, but because of the hardness of people's hearts, God allowed servitude and slavery, but He gave guidelines to govern it. From these verses do you believe the creditor had the right to take the widow's sons?

3. How did God, through Elisha, meet the widow's need? (2 Kings 4:2-7)

4. No matter what our circumstances are, or what problems we face, God will meet our needs if we will only trust and obey Him. What do you learn about this in the following verses?

   Matthew 6:26-33

   Ephesians 3:20-21

   1 Peter 5:6-7

5. Elisha, as a man of God, was just as available to help this poor widow as he had been available to help the kings in 2 Kings 3. Read James 2:1-9. How are believers today to be like Elisha in this way?

6. Personal: When you face a crisis, to whom do you turn for help? How has God helped you in the past when you put your trust in Him?

Fifth Day: Review 2 Kings 3-4, concentrating on 4:8-37.

1. How did the woman of Shunem use her position and possessions to promote the work of God? (2 Kings 4:8-10)

2. a. How did Elisha show his appreciation? (2 Kings 4:11-16a)

    b. From the woman's response in 2 Kings 4:16b and her later words in 2 Kings 4:28, do you think she wanted a child?

3. Just as Elisha said, she gave birth to a son. When the woman's son grew older, what happened to him? (2 Kings 4:17-20)

4. By faith, to whom did the woman turn for help? (2 Kings 4:21-28; summarize briefly)

5. a. When Gehazi's mission carried out at Elisha's command was ineffective, what did Elisha do? (2 Kings 4:29-36; summarize briefly)

    b. Challenge: Compare Elisha's symbolic actions to his teacher Elijah's in 1 Kings 17:17-24.

6. Personal: The woman of Shunem, in her desire to help Elisha, "a holy man of God" (2 Kings 4:9), used her gifts to promote the work of God. New Testament believers are also to do this, "so that in all things God may be praised through Jesus Christ" (see 1 Peter 4:9-11). Hospitality, opening your home and life to others, is something anyone can do.[1] How is the Lord calling you to promote His work?

Sixth Day: Review 2 Kings 3-4, concentrating on 4:38-44.

1. a. Elisha could have remained comfortably in Shunem, but where did he go instead, and what was the situation there? (2 Kings 4:38a)

   b. In spite of the situation in that region, what did Elisha instruct his servant to do for these prophets? (2 Kings 4:38b)

2. a. What did one of the prophets do, and what was the result? (2 Kings 4:39-40)

   b. How did God work through Elisha to make the stew edible? (2 Kings 4:41)

3. Challenge: Flour, in and of itself, does not remove poison from food. Compare this to the miracle 2 Kings 2:21. Why do you believe the flour made the stew edible?

4. a. What did the man from Baal Shalishah bring to Elisha? (2 Kings 4:42a)

   b. What was Elisha's servant's objection when he was commanded to give it to the prophets to eat? (2 Kings 4:42b-43a)

5. a. What did the Lord promise through Elisha? Was the promise fulfilled? (2 Kings 4:43b-44)

   b. Challenge: How was this miracle similar to the work of Jesus in Matthew 14:15-21?

6. Personal: God has promised to supply all the needs of His people, both physical and spiritual (see Ephesians 3:20; Philippians 4:19). Our responsibility is to trust Him and obey His commands. What are some things for which you need to trust the Lord today? Perhaps you struggle with a personal weakness or failure, with physical or financial needs, or with a difficult relationship. Do you believe that God is able to meet these needs? If you aren't sure, you may want to pray as the man prayed in Mark 9:24, "...I do believe; help me overcome my unbelief!"

---

1. For ideas, see *You Can Do It Too! Opening Your Heart and Home to Share God's Love*, by Doris W. Greig, available from Joy of Living.

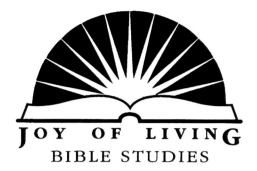

2 Kings
Lesson 3

JOY OF LIVING
BIBLE STUDIES

2 Kings Chapters 3-4

Setting: The Northern Kingdom of Israel

In the last lesson, we briefly met Joram,[1] the new king of the northern kingdom of Israel, who rose to the throne after the death of his brother, Ahaziah. Now, in 2 Kings 3:2-3, we read an evaluation of his reign: "He did evil in the eyes of the Lord, but not as his father and mother had done. He got rid of the sacred stone of Baal that his father had made. Nevertheless he clung to the sins of Jeroboam son of Nebat, which he had caused Israel to commit; he did not turn away from them."

Joram's father, Ahab, had built in Samaria a temple to Baal for his wife, Jezebel (see 1 Kings 16:32-33). Apparently a stone representation of Baal was placed in this temple. Joram, to his credit, got rid of this sacred stone. However, he didn't go far enough in removing apostasy from his kingdom. He left in place the golden calves, with their altars and false prophets, which King Jeroboam had set up in Bethel and Dan for his people to worship (see 1 Kings 12:26-33).

The Campaign Against Moab

Many years prior to this time, King David had conquered Moab, an area east of the Jordan River. After the northern kingdom of Israel broke away from the southern kingdom of Judah, Israel apparently continued the domination of Moab. After the death of King Ahab, Moab saw its chance and broke free of subjugation to Israel.

Ahab's son, Ahaziah, had been unable to overcome Moab's rebellion during his two-year reign. Because Ahaziah had no son, upon his death his brother, Joram, became king. Now, during King Joram's reign, Mesha, king of Moab, refused to pay to Israel the burdensome tribute of a hundred thousand lambs and the wool of a hundred thousand rams. Joram wasn't going to take this lying down. He mobilized his forces and sent a message to Jehoshaphat, king of Judah, asking for his help in the fight against Moab.

Jehoshaphat agreed to join with Joram, for a number of possible reasons:

- The two kings were relatives: Jehoshaphat's son (and co-regent), Jehoram, was married to Joram's aunt, Athaliah.

- Although Jehoshaphat had previously been condemned by prophets of the Lord for his alliances with the northern kings Ahab and Ahaziah (see 2 Chronicles 18-20), he may have considered Joram less evil than his predecessors, since he had gotten rid of the sacred stone of Baal.

- Jehoshaphat's kingdom of Judah had been attacked previously by the Moabites (see 2 Chronicles 20). Now, he may have been disturbed by the potential danger to Judah from the increasingly strong Moabites.

When Joram asked Jehoshaphat's advice in planning the expedition, Jehoshaphat proposed a route through Edom (see map on page 8). The Edomites, being subject to Judah,[2] could not veto this plan, and would in fact join forces with the armies of Israel and Judah in the attack. Their route through the Desert of Edom led the allied armies south of the Dead Sea, giving them the advantage of surprise, since they would not attack Moab's main fortifications in the north. In addition, this route would not allow the armies of Aram to easily come to Moab's aid by attacking the allies from the rear.

Elisha Is Consulted

But the campaign did not go as planned. After marching "roundabout" for a week in the desert, the armies had run out of water for themselves and for their animals. Joram was terrified, convinced that they would certainly be overcome by Moab. But Jehoshaphat asked to consult a true prophet of the Lord. One of Jehoshaphat's officers reported that the prophet Elisha was available. Unlike Ahaziah's peremptory summons to Elisha, "Man of God...Come down!" (2 Kings 1:6), the three allied kings themselves "went down to" Elisha.

Elisha immediately addressed Joram, saying, "Why do you want to involve me? Go to the prophets of your father and the prophets of your mother" (2 Kings 3:13). But, out of respect for the godly King Jehoshaphat of Judah, Elisha promised to consult the Lord on their behalf.

Elisha called for a harpist, perhaps to create an atmosphere of peace and quietness, conducive to receiving the word of the Lord. Then he received God's message, which he relayed to the kings: "I will fill this valley with pools of water...You will see neither wind nor rain, yet this valley will be filled with water, and you, your cattle and your

---

1. Some Bible versions call him "Jehoram." See footnote on page 11.

2. The "king of Edom" was in reality a governor appointed by Jehoshaphat (see 1 Kings 22:47).

other animals will drink. This is an easy thing in the eyes of the Lord; he will also deliver Moab into your hands" (2 Kings 3:16-18).

God's word given through Elisha was fulfilled. Water ran down out of the mountains of Edom, rescuing the thirsty armies of Israel, Judah, and Edom, and their animals. But the same waters that spelled life for the allies, spelled death for the Moabites. Mistaking the water that gleamed red in the light of the rising sun for blood, Moab thought the attacking armies must have slaughtered each other, and rushed to the armies' campsite to seize the plunder. The allied armies fought against Moab until Moab turned and ran away. The Israelites followed and invaded Moab, causing great destruction.

The king of Moab was desperate. He tried to break through to the king of Edom, perhaps hoping Edom would turn and stand with him against Israel and Judah. When that failed, he sacrificed his firstborn son and heir as a burnt offering to the Moabite god Chemosh, attempting to get his god to come to his aid.

Second Kings 3:27 concludes, "And there came great wrath against Israel. And they withdrew from him and returned to their own land." One commentator says of this, "Sickened by the maddened spectacle of senseless human sacrifice, the allies lifted the siege and returned to their homes."[1] Another suggests, "It seems that just when total victory appeared to be in Israel's grasp, God's displeasure with the Ahab dynasty showed itself in some way that caused the Israelite kings to give up the campaign."[2] Whatever the reason, the campaign was ended. The rebellion of Moab had been suppressed.

The Widow's Olive Oil

Second Kings chapter four continues the description of Elisha's ministry and miracles. The widow of one of the prophets of the Lord came to Elisha for help. The creditor for a debt that she was unable to pay was insisting on taking her two sons as his slaves to repay the debt. The creditor was within his rights under Mosaic Law, though the law limited the term of bondage and required the slaves to be treated as hired workers.[3] But imagine how this poor woman felt, having already lost her husband, at the thought of also losing her two boys.

Elisha, with compassion, asked her, "What shall I do for you?" Finding out that she had nothing of value except a small flask of olive oil, he told her to borrow as many empty jars from her neighbors as possible. Then she was to go into her house and close the door, and pour oil into all the jars. The woman obeyed, and as her boys helped her with the jars, the oil kept pouring from her flask until all the borrowed jars were filled. Elisha told her to sell the oil and pay her debts, and use the remaining money to live on.

What a striking example of faithful obedience, one step at a time, bringing bountiful blessings. When you are faced with a problem or a decision, take it to the Lord just as the poor woman took her problem to Elisha. Then, as He gives you direction, whether through His Word, through circumstances, through wise counsel from another believer,

or through the still, small voice of His Holy Spirit within you, obey Him one step at a time. You may not be able to see how obeying that one step will solve your problem, but it will certainly take you in the right direction. It is often only after we have taken the first step of faith that we are able to see the next step.

The Shunammite's Son

As Elisha traveled around in ministry, he often went through the town of Shunem. He frequently stopped at the home of a well-to-do couple to eat with them. At the wife's suggestion, the husband made and furnished a small room on the roof for Elisha to stay in whenever he came.

This reminds me of my family's experiences when I was growing up. My mother, Doris Greig (Joy of Living's founder), was known for her hospitality. She and my father often hosted missionaries, pastors, and many others for meals and as houseguests.[4] We kids never knew who might appear at the dinner table on any particular evening. It was a real learning experience to hear our visitors talk about their homes in other cities, states, or countries, their ministries, and their appreciation for the home-cooked meal.

We are instructed in Hebrews 13:2, "Do not forget to show hospitality to strangers, for by so doing some people have shown hospitality to angels without knowing it." Then in Galatians 6:10 we are told, "As we have opportunity, let us do good to all people, especially to those who belong to the family of believers." And finally in Matthew 25:40 the Lord says, "Truly I tell you, whatever you did for one of the least of these brothers and sisters of mine, you did for me."

You may not be in a situation where you can invite people into your home, or you may not be comfortable with it, but there are many ways to be obedient to these verses. In her book, *You Can Do It, Too!* Doris Greig shares many easy, practical ways to open your heart and home to share God's love with others.

God's Gracious Intervention

On one occasion, Elisha asked the Shunnamite woman how he might repay her kindness to him. She said she had no special needs. After she had departed, Elisha's servant, Gehazi, pointed out that the woman was childless and that her husband was old. In that day, a widow with no children faced a future with no protector or provider; children were her only hope for "social security" in her old age. Elisha told Gehazi to call the woman. He then promised her, "About this time next year...you will hold a son in your arms" (2 Kings 4:16). And so it came to pass, through God's gracious intervention.

One day, when the child was older, he was with his father in the fields with the reapers. The boy became suddenly and critically ill, and he died in his mother's arms the same day. She laid him on the bed in the room they had built for Elisha, and immediately set out toward

---

1. *The Expositors Bible Commentary*, notes on 2 Kings 3:26-27.
2. *NIV Study Notes* on 2 Kings 3:27.
3. Ibid, notes on 2 Kings 4:1.

4. Doris W. Greig, *You Can Do It, Too! Opening Your Heart and Home to Share God's Love*, available from Joy of Living.

Mount Carmel, about 20 miles away,[1] to find the prophet. Elisha saw her coming and sent Gehazi to meet her and find out what was wrong, but the woman would not confide in the servant. She went straight to Elisha and fell at his feet to pour out her distress.

Elisha sent Gehazi to run to the woman's house and lay Elisha's staff on the boy's face. Apparently Elisha expected the Lord to restore the boy's life, not by a "magic" staff, but by the staff as a representation of Elisha's presence and as a symbol of divine power.[2] But the woman insisted that Elisha himself come back to her home. Gehazi went back to meet Elisha and reported that the boy had not "awakened."

So Elisha himself went into the rooftop room, shut the door, and prayed to the Lord. He followed his prayer with the symbolic action of laying himself facedown on the boy's body. Perhaps he learned this through his teacher Elijah's experience with the son of the widow of Zarephath. In that case, Elijah had "stretched himself out on the boy three times and cried out to the Lord, 'Lord my God, let this boy's life return to him!' The Lord heard Elijah's cry, and the boy's life returned to him, and he lived" (1 Kings 17:21-22). The Lord also heard Elisha's prayer and restored the life of the Shunnamite woman's son.

When we offer hospitality to God's servants, we may not experience personal miracles such as the Shunnamite woman did. But we will receive God's blessings for faithful service to Him and to His people—fellowship, joy, and spiritual growth and fulfillment. Watch for the opportunities God gives you to open your life and your home to others.

Further Miracles

Second Kings chapter 4 closes with two incidents that took place in the religious community, known as the company of the prophets,[3] at Gilgal. At the time, there was a famine in that region. When Elisha returned to Gilgal, he instructed his servant to prepare a large pot of stew for the prophets. One of the students went out to gather herbs for the stew. He found wild gourds, and picked as many as he could carry, certainly congratulating himself for such a wonderful discovery. He returned and cut them up into the pot of stew, "though no one knew what they were."

When the men began to eat the stew, they cried out to Elisha, "Man of God, there is death in the pot!" Elisha called for some flour, and stirred it into the pot. This time, when the men ate, "there was nothing harmful in the pot." The flour itself didn't make the stew edible. Rather, it was a sign of Elisha's faith that the Lord would provide nourishment for them, even during a time of famine.

I know of a man who was a poor coal-miner during the 1920's through the early 1950's. He and his wife were blessed with many children. While he worked in the mines she cared for the family at home, tending the garden, baking bread, raising chickens and rabbits, and all the chores you would expect on a small farm. She became very ill, and they feared she would die. Not only was the man concerned that the woman he loved would die, but who would run their small farm and care for the children while he worked? As he sat in their kitchen, planning to fry some potatoes for the children's dinner, the still small voice of the Lord spoke to him, saying, "If you were the right man, that potato could heal her." He knew that God was asking him to trust Him as never before. He cut up the potato and made potato soup from it with nothing but the potato, some milk and some salt and pepper. He spooned it into his wife's mouth and from that day she began to recover. There was nothing special about the potato or the other ingredients; what was special was that the man acted by faith, in obedience to God's instruction. He was a changed man. He walked with the Lord the rest of his life, and died with the name of His Savior on his lips.

Hebrews 11:6 says, "Without faith it is impossible to please God, because anyone who comes to him must believe that he exists and that he rewards those who earnestly seek him." God does not always heal; God does not always do what we think is best. However, He asks us to have faith in Him, faith that He is who He says He is—that He is all powerful, that He is all knowing, and that He loves us and will always do what is best for those who put their faith in Him. He will guide, He will lead, and He will bring us into an ever-deepening relationship with Himself.

The second incident involved 20 loaves of barley bread baked from the first ripe grain, along with some heads of new grain, that a man brought to Elisha. The people of Israel had been instructed to bring the first fruits of each new harvest to the priests in the temple in Jerusalem (see Deuteronomy 18:3-5). Rather than bring these offerings to Israel's false priests at Bethel and Dan, godly people in the northern kingdom may have contributed their offerings to Elisha and the other true prophets of the Lord.

Elisha ordered that the bread be given to the prophets. His servant asked how to distribute it, since it was obviously insufficient to feed the 100 men. Elisha answered with this word from the Lord, "They will eat and have some left over" (2 Kings 4:43). And, again, so it came to pass.

Just as these believers in the true God were sustained by His loving care, we too are to look to Him for our daily needs. Jesus taught us to pray, "Give us today our daily bread" (Matthew 6:11). Have you put your trust in Him for everything you need each day—housing, food, clothing, peace, joy, etc.? Is there some current need that worries you? Why not pray about it now?

---

1. M.G. Easton, *Easton's Bible Dictionary*, "Shunem".
2. *NIV Study Notes* on 2 Kings 4:29.
3. "This phrase is traditionally rendered 'sons of the prophets,' but the Hebrew for 'sons' here refers to members of a group, not to male children. Companies of prophets were apparently religious communities that sprang up in the face of general indifference and apostasy for the purpose of mutual edification and the cultivation of the experience of God." (*NIV Study Bible Notes* on 1 Kings 20:35)

Study Questions

Before you begin your study this week:
- ❧ Pray and ask God to speak to you through His Holy Spirit.
- ❧ Use only the Bible for your answers.
- ❧ Write down your answers and the verses you used.
- ❧ Answer the "Challenge" questions if you have the time and want to do them.
- ❧ Share your answers to the "Personal" questions with the class only if you want to share them.

First Day: Read the Commentary on 2 Kings 3-4.

1. What meaningful or new thought did you find in the Commentary on 2 Kings 3-4 or from your teacher's lecture?

2. Look for a verse in the lesson to memorize this week. Write it down, carry it with you, or post it in a prominent place. Make a real effort to learn the verse and its "address" (reference of where it is found in the Bible).

Second Day: Read 2 Kings 5:1—6:7, concentrating on 5:1-6.

1. a. From 2 Kings 5:1, who was Naaman, and what problem did he face?

   b. To whom did the writer of 2 Kings give credit for Naaman's success in battle? (2 Kings 5:1)

   c. Challenge: The people of Aram did not worship "the LORD," the God of Israel, yet the writer of 2 Kings made this amazing statement! How is the sovereignty of God over *all* nations, not just over Israel, demonstrated in Ezekiel 30:24 and Amos 9:7, for example?

2. a. How did a young Israelite girl happen to be serving in Naaman's household? (2 Kings 5:2)

   b. What did she tell her mistress? (2 Kings 5:3)

3. a. What did Naaman do when he heard this? (2 Kings 5:4)

   b. What was his king's reaction? (2 Kings 5:5a)

4. a. What did Naaman take with him when he went to find the prophet in Israel? (2 Kings 5:5b)

    b. Challenge: Read 1 Kings 16:24 to get an idea of the relative value of the silver Naaman carried.

5. What did the king of Aram write to the king of Israel? How had he misunderstood the message of the Israelite girl? (2 Kings 5:6)

6. Personal: Think about the Israelite girl's situation. In spite of her difficult circumstances, she believed in the Lord's power and goodness and was willing to share this knowledge with her captors. What is your attitude towards God when you find yourself in "bad" circumstances? Do you still tell others about His power and goodness?

Third Day: Review 2 Kings 5:1—6:7, concentrating on 5:7-14.

1. How did the king of Israel react when he read the letter Naaman carried from the king of Aram? (2 Kings 5:7)

2. a. When Elisha heard of this, what did he do? (2 Kings 5:8)

    b. Challenge: Review 2 Kings 3:1-3, 13-14. Why do you think that the king of Israel himself did not suggest that Naaman visit Elisha?

3. What did Elisha do when Naaman went to visit him? (2 Kings 5:9-10)

4. What was Naaman's reaction? (2 Kings 5:11-12)

5. a. How did Naaman's servants counsel him? (2 Kings 5:13)

    b. What happened when he followed Elisha's instructions? (2 Kings 5:14)

6. Personal: Leprosy was a terrible disease, and at that time there was no known cure for it. Naaman traveled to Israel ready to pay for his healing, but God neither needed nor wanted Naaman's money. God did not cleanse Naaman of leprosy until Naaman humbled himself and, by faith, acted in obedience to God's instructions for being cleansed given through Elisha. God is not impressed by a person's wealth or importance in the eyes of the world. He tells us that we are all hopeless sinners, needing to be cleansed of our sin, but unable to do so ourselves. He, however, has made a way for us to be cleansed through the blood of Jesus Christ. By faith we must humbly accept that Jesus Christ paid the price for our sin on the cross. He did it all for us. Have you believed what God said in the Bible about your sinfulness and placed your faith in Jesus Christ's death and resurrection to cleanse you of sin and give you new life? If you haven't previously done this, won't you do it now? Turn to page 4 for more information, or you may want to speak to your pastor, Bible study leader, or another Christian leader.

Fourth Day: Review 2 Kings 5:1—6:7, concentrating on 5:15-19a.

1. What did Naaman now know from his experience? (2 Kings 5:15a)

2. a. What did he want to do for Elisha? (2 Kings 5:15b)

   b. What was Elisha's response? (2 Kings 5:16)

3. What did Naaman ask, so that he would have a place in Aram to worship the Lord?[1] (2 Kings 5:17)

4. a. What was Naaman's concern about his official duties in Aram? (2 Kings 5:18)

   b. Elisha did not directly address Naaman's concern, which was an issue solely between Naaman and the Lord. With what blessing did Elisha send Naaman away? (2 Kings 5:19a)

5. Challenge: Read in Matthew 10:8 Jesus' instructions to the twelve disciples that He sent out to preach to the "lost sheep of Israel" (verse 6). How was the disciples' service in His name to flow out of what He had done for them? How is this similar to Elisha's refusal of Naaman's gift?

6. Personal: Do you serve the Lord out of an overflowing heart of gratitude to Him, or do you expect something in return from people that you serve in His name? You may not expect financial gifts, but perhaps you have been disappointed when you didn't receive recognition or praise for your service. Are you willing to do what God asks even if no one else seems to notice or care? How does this apply to a situation you have experienced, or are currently experiencing?

---

1. "In the ancient world it was commonly thought that a deity could be worshiped only on the soil of the nation to which he was bound." (*The NIV Study Bible Notes* on 2 Kings 5:17)

Fifth Day: Review 2 Kings 5:1—6:7, concentrating on 5:19b-27.

1. What did Gehazi, Elisha's servant, decide to do? (2 Kings 5:19b-20)

2. a. How did Naaman receive Gehazi? (2 Kings 5:21)

   b. Contrast Naaman's action and words in 2 Kings 5:21 with the way he was described earlier in this chapter before he was healed (see 2 Kings 5:1,9,11-12).

3. a. What story did Gehazi make up? (2 Kings 5:22)

   b. How did Naaman respond? (2 Kings 5:23)

4. a. How did Gehazi try to hide his actions from Elisha? (2 Kings 5:24-25)

   b. Did he fool Elisha? (2 Kings 5:26)

   c. Challenge: What do you learn from the following verses about the possibility of hiding our sins from God?

      Numbers 32:23

      Psalm 90:8

      1 Corinthians 4:5

5. What consequences did Gehazi suffer for his deception and greed? (2 Kings 5:27)

6. Personal: Are you trying to hide your sin? You may be able to fool the people around you, but no one can fool God. What does 1 John 1:9-10 tell us to do when we have sinned? Every follower of Christ needs to do this regularly. Why not pray about this now?

Sixth Day: Review 2 Kings 5:1—6:7, concentrating on 6:1-7.

1. What problem did the company of the prophets of the Lord face, and what solution did they suggest? (2 Kings 6:1-2)

2. What did they ask Elisha to do? (2 Kings 6:3)

3. What happened while they were working? (2 Kings 6:4-5)

4. At that time an iron axe-head was a costly tool, too expensive for the members of their group to purchase. If the borrower lost it, he would have to work off the value as a bondservant.[1] How did the Lord, through Elisha, demonstrate His concern for the welfare of his faithful prophets? (2 Kings 6:6-7)

5. God is always concerned for the welfare of every one of His faithful followers. How did Jesus express this in Luke 12:6-7, 24-28?

6. Personal: What problem or problems are you worrying about? Do you think those things are outside of God's area of concern? How would your attitude and emotions change if you truly believed Jesus' words in Luke 12? Why not pray about this now?

---

1. *NIV Study Bible Notes* on 2 Kings 6:5.

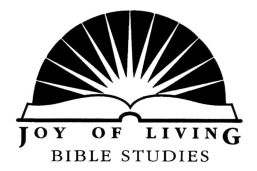

2 Kings
Lesson 4

JOY OF LIVING
BIBLE STUDIES

2 Kings Chapters 5:1—6:7

Setting: The Northern Kingdom of Israel

Second Kings chapter 5 opens with a description of a new character, who was not an Israelite—Naaman, the commander of the army of the king of Aram. Aram was located to the northeast of the kingdom of Israel. Israel had suffered periodic warfare with Aram throughout its history. Although at this time the two nations were officially at peace, bands of Aramean raiders still invaded Israel from time to time.

Naaman is described as "a great man in the sight of his master and highly regarded...a valiant soldier" (2 Kings 5:1). The writer of Kings gives an interesting reason for the success of this commanding officer: "because through him the LORD had given victory to Aram." What a telling illustration of the sovereignty of God: He controls the fate of all nations, not just of His chosen people, Israel.

Naaman faced a big problem. In spite of his military victories and the high regard of his king, Naaman suffered from leprosy, an incurable, serious disease. Dr. Allen Gillen describes leprosy:

Leprosy has terrified humanity since ancient times...The precise meaning of the leprosy in both the Old and New Testaments is still in dispute, but it probably includes the modern Hansen's disease (especially in the New Testament) and infectious skin diseases...For many centuries, leprosy was considered a curse of God, often associated with sin. It did not kill, but neither did it seem to end. Instead, it lingered for years, causing the tissues to degenerate and deforming the body...Patients with leprosy experience disfigurement of the skin and bones, twisting of the limbs, and curling of the fingers...The largest number of deformities develop from loss of pain sensation due to extensive nerve damage. For instance, inattentive patients can pick up a cup of boiling water without flinching...People with leprosy traditionally suffered banishment from family and neighbors.[1]

Naaman's leprosy must have been observable, or at least was well known to his entire household. Even the young Israelite servant girl, who had been taken captive by Aramean raiders and given or sold to Naaman, knew of his illness. She said to her mistress, "If only my master would see the prophet who is in Samaria! He would cure him of his leprosy" (2 Kings 5:2). Just think of what this girl's attitude

demonstrated. Although she was a young girl who had been stolen from her family and pressed into servitude in a strange land, she held on to her faith in the God she knew worked through His servant Elisha. She unreservedly shared this knowledge with her captors. Would you be as faithful to your Lord and as generous in sharing knowledge of His power with someone who had caused you great harm or sorrow?

When Naaman heard of the Israelite prophet who could heal him, he went to his king with the news. The king, who "highly regarded" Naaman, offered to send a letter to the king of Israel. Perhaps the king of Aram assumed that the Israelite prophet would be subject to the authority of Israel's king, and believed a word from the king would gain Naaman quicker access to the prophet or make it more likely that Naaman would be healed. Or this may have been political protocol: for the leader of the army of Aram to venture into the territory of Israel might have appeared to be an act of aggression if prior notice was not given. It also could have been a demand with a veiled threat—that if Naaman's healing wasn't accomplished, there would be trouble.

Naaman traveled to Israel, taking along extravagant gifts—ten talents (about 750 pounds) of silver, six thousand shekels (about 150 pounds) of gold, and ten changes of clothing.[2] The letter he carried from his king to Israel's king said, "With this letter I am sending my servant Naaman to you so that you may cure him of his leprosy" (2 Kings 5:6). What a shock was in store for Israel's King Joram.[3]

Naaman Visits Elisha

Naaman may have approached King Joram with hope for a cure, and yet also with a certain arrogance, as commander of the army of what he must have considered a superior power. From the way the text reads it appears that Naaman was not in Joram's presence when the letter was read. Upon reading the letter, Joram "tore his robes and said, 'Am I God? Can I kill and bring back to life? Why does this fellow send someone to me to be cured of his leprosy? See how he is trying to pick a quarrel with me'" (2 Kings 5:7).

The letter apparently didn't mention the prophet Elisha, and Joram felt that he was being put into an impossible situation. He thought

---

1. Dr. Alan Gillen, "Biblical Leprosy: Shedding Light on the Disease that Shuns," *Answers Magazine*, June 10, 2007.

2. Equivalent weights in pounds are from *NIV Study Notes* on 2 Kings 5:5. For an idea of the relative value of the silver Naaman carried, 1 Kings 16:24 says that when Omri, an earlier Israelite king, purchased the hill of Samaria, where he built the city of Samaria about 30 years earlier, he paid only 2 talents of silver.

3. Some Bible versions call him "Jehoram." See footnote on page 11.

the king of Aram was trying to manufacture a reason for a declaration of war against Israel. That might be understandable, and yet it also shows how Joram's thoughts traveled only on an earthly plane. He apparently didn't even consider turning to God, or to His prophet Elisha, for help and counsel.

News traveled fast, and Elisha soon heard the whole story. He sent a message to Joram, "Why have you torn your robes? Have the man come to me and he will know that there is a prophet in Israel" (2 Kings 5:8).

So Naaman went to Elisha's house. It must have been quite a sight, all the horses and chariots, the soldiers and servants—the entire retinue of an important man. Elisha was not impressed. He did not even go out to meet Naaman, but sent a messenger to say to him, "Go, wash yourself seven times in the Jordan, and your flesh will be restored and you will be cleansed" (2 Kings 5:10).

Naaman was insulted and outraged. He thought Elisha should have come to him in person, calling on the Lord his God and waving his hands over him, to cure him of his leprosy. Instead, Elisha had not even deigned to show himself, and he had instructed Naaman to wash in the Jordan River, which was unimpressive and muddy compared with the rivers of Naaman's home in Damascus.

Elisha, however, did not use magic techniques and formulas to heal. Only the Lord his God had the power to heal. Naaman needed to obey the word of the Lord's prophet. One of Naaman's servants offered wise advice, "My father, if the prophet had told you to do some great thing, would you not have done it? How much more, then, when he tells you, 'Wash and be cleansed'!" (2 Kings 5:13). And, just as Elisha promised, when Naaman obeyed God's word by dipping in the Jordan seven times, he received complete healing.

Leprosy was a terrible disease, and at that time there was no known cure for it. Naaman had traveled to Israel ready to pay for his healing, but God neither needed nor wanted Naaman's money. God, through Elisha, offered Naaman the gift of being cleansed of leprosy. All Naaman had to do was humble himself and accept the gift in the way it was being offered—that is by dipping seven times in the Jordan. When Naaman finally did, then and only then was Naaman cleansed.

God is not impressed by a person's wealth or importance in the eyes of the world. He tells us that we are all hopeless sinners, needing to be cleansed of our sin, but unable to do so ourselves. We cannot earn or purchase our cleansing by what we give or what we do. God, thankfully, has made a way for us to be cleansed. Just as Naaman had to receive his cleansing from leprosy in the manner God set forth, so we must receive our cleansing from sin in the manner God set forth. By faith, each of us must humbly accept that Jesus Christ paid the price for our sin on the cross. He paid it all for us; we cannot add to what Jesus did. It is by faith alone in what Jesus did that we are cleansed from our sin (see Ephesians 2:8-9).

Have you believed what God said in the Bible about your sinfulness and placed your faith in Jesus Christ's death and resurrection to cleanse you of sin and give you new life? If you haven't previously done this, won't you do it now? Turn to page 4 for more information, or you may want to speak to your pastor, Bible study leader, or another Christian leader.

There are other situations in life in which God asks us to act by faith, in obedience to what He has said in His Word. Maybe you, too, are facing a frightening problem—perhaps an illness, a troubled marriage, a rebellious child, or the loss of a job. What is God asking you to do? One of the following Scriptures may remind you of His command for you in your particular situation:

- "'Do not seek revenge or bear a grudge against anyone among your people, but love your neighbor as yourself. I am the Lord." (Leviticus 19:18)

- "Be still before the Lord and wait patiently for him; do not fret when people succeed in their ways, when they carry out their wicked schemes. Refrain from anger and turn from wrath; do not fret —it leads only to evil." (Psalm 37:7-8)

- "Trust in the Lord with all your heart and lean not on your own understanding; in all your ways submit to him, and he will make your paths straight." (Proverbs 3:5-6)

- "A new command I give you: Love one another. As I have loved you, so you must love one another." (John 13:34)

- "Love is patient, love is kind. It does not envy, it does not boast, it is not proud. It does not dishonor others, it is not self-seeking, it is not easily angered, it keeps no record of wrongs." (1 Corinthians 13:4-5)

- "Bear with each other and forgive one another if any of you has a grievance against someone. Forgive as the Lord forgave you." (Colossians 3:13)

- "Do not repay evil with evil or insult with insult. On the contrary, repay evil with blessing, because to this you were called so that you may inherit a blessing." (1 Peter 3:9)

- "Anyone who claims to be in the light but hates a brother or sister is still in the darkness. Anyone who loves their brother and sister lives in the light, and there is nothing in them to make them stumble." (1 John 2:9-10)

- "If anyone has material possessions and sees a brother or sister in need but has no pity on them, how can the love of God be in that person? Dear children, let us not love with words or speech but with actions and in truth." (1 John 3:17-18)

When we obey God's Word, we receive the gift of His grace. He may not make our problems go away, but He will enable us to rise above them, to live in His peace and joy in spite of our circumstances. And He will use all of them for our good and for His glory (see Romans 8:28-29).

Naaman's Confession

Naaman returned to Elisha and told him, "Now I know that there is no God in all the world except in Israel" (2 Kings 5:15). What a confession! He realized that he could no longer worship any other god but

Yahweh, unlike the Israelites of the northern kingdom, who constantly wavered between the worship of the Lord, the worship of the golden calf idols set up by Jeroboam son of Nebat, and the worship of Baal. Following this confession, Naaman continued, "So please accept a gift from your servant." But Elisha would not accept a thing, in spite of Naaman's continued urging. He didn't seek monetary rewards for proclaiming the word of the Lord, and if he accepted the gift from Naaman, it may have clouded the fact that Naaman's cleansing was a gift from God and not an exchange of favors.

Then Naaman asked if he could take two mule-loads of soil from Israel back to his home in Aram.[1] On this imported Israelite ground, Naaman would make burnt offerings and sacrifices to the Lord God of Israel.

Finally, Naaman asked Elisha in advance for the Lord's forgiveness for the fact that when he entered the temple of Rimmon with his master, the king of Aram, he would have to bow down because the king was leaning on his arm. Naaman, though a true believer, felt it necessary to continue to carry out his official responsibilities in his pagan homeland. Elisha did not directly address Naaman's question, but commended him to the leading and grace of God, saying, "Go in peace."

Gehazi's Greed

After Naaman left, Elisha's servant Gehazi couldn't get all those rich gifts out of his mind. He couldn't understand why Elisha had allowed "this Aramean" to get off so easily. The Arameans had long been enemies of Israel. In fact, Naaman had learned of the existence of Elisha from a young girl the Arameans had stolen from Israel. So Gehazi hurried down the road after Naaman. When Naaman saw him coming, he stopped and got down from his chariot to meet him. What a change in Naaman this indicates. He was no longer the proud and arrogant man who was insulted when Elisha sent a servant to speak to him. Now, in humility, he came down from his place of honor on the chariot to meet the servant, asking, "Is everything all right?" (2 Kings 5:21).

Gehazi made up a story about why Elisha needed some of Naaman's gifts after all. He asked Naaman for a talent of silver and two sets of clothing for two young men who had just arrived from the company of prophets in the hill country of Ephraim. Naaman generously insisted that he take two talents of silver with the clothing. He gave the bags of silver to two of his servants to carry for Gehazi, who secretly concealed them in the house until he could retrieve them later.

When Gehazi later went in to Elisha, the prophet confronted him with what God had revealed to him of Gehazi's greed and deception. Just as Gehazi could not conceal his sin from Elisha, so we cannot conceal our sin from God. First Corinthians 4:5 says, "He will bring to light what is hidden in darkness and will expose the motives of the heart." We may think that no one sees what we are doing, and that nobody knows what we're really thinking, but we're just fooling ourselves. God is omniscient—He knows everything, at all times.

Elisha announced Gehazi's punishment—he and his descendants would suffer from the leprosy from which Naaman had been healed. He was banished in disgrace from Elisha's presence. Although he had served as Elisha's trusted aide, his true character was revealed by his actions during this time of testing.

We, too, are tested by the events and circumstances we encounter each day. The way we respond to temptations and trials reveals our true character. The apostle Peter wrote, "In this you rejoice, though now for a little while, if necessary, you have been grieved by various trials, so that the tested genuineness of your faith—more precious than gold that perishes though it is tested by fire—may be found to result in praise and glory and honor at the revelation of Jesus Christ" (1 Peter 1:6-7). Has your faith been revealed as genuine when you were tested? If not, or if you're not sure, pray and ask God's forgiveness for your sin, and ask Him to strengthen your faith.

Faithfulness Is Rewarded

At the end of 2 Kings 5, Elisha's servant Gehazi received the consequences of his unfaithfulness. In contrast, in chapter 6, we see how God rewarded the faithfulness of His prophets.

Several companies or schools of prophets were established in the northern kingdom of Israel, located in Bethel, Jericho, and Gilgal. The company in 2 Kings 6 was apparently in Jericho, which is near the Jordan River. The prophets there found that the place they met for instruction was too small, and suggested to Elisha that they go to the Jordan, where they could obtain building supplies and build a new meeting place. Elisha agreed that this would be wise, and also agreed to go with them to the work site.

As one of them cut down a tree, the iron ax head came apart from its handle and fell into the river. The prophet was horrified, because it was borrowed. At that time, an iron ax head was an expensive tool, and the prophetic students probably could not afford to purchase a replacement. The borrower might have had to work off its value as a bondservant.[2]

The student asked Elisha's help, and, through God's power, Elisha caused the submerged ax head to float so that the man could retrieve it. Elisha's action in cutting the stick and throwing it where the ax head fell is not significant in itself. It was just the vehicle for the Lord to work a miracle on behalf of his faithful prophets.

God is just as concerned for your welfare as He was for that of his Old Testament prophets. He has unique ways of meeting every need and concern that we bring to Him. Have you learned to rely on Him?

---

1. Possibly this was because Naaman thought that a god could be worshipped only on the soil of the nation to which he was bound. (*NIV Study Notes* on 2 Kings 5:17)

2. *NIV Study Notes* on 2 Kings 6:5.

Study Questions

Before you begin your study this week:
- Pray and ask God to speak to you through His Holy Spirit.
- Use only the Bible for your answers.
- Write down your answers and the verses you used.
- Answer the "Challenge" questions if you have the time and want to do them.
- Share your answers to the "Personal" questions with the class only if you want to share them.

First Day: Read the Commentary on 2 Kings 5:1—6:7.

1. What meaningful or new thought did you find in the Commentary on 2 Kings 5:1—6:7 or from your teacher's lecture?

2. Look for a verse in the lesson to memorize this week. Write it down, carry it with you, or post it in a prominent place. Make a real effort to learn the verse and its "address" (reference of where it is found in the Bible).

Second Day: Read 2 Kings 6:8—7:20, concentrating on 6:8-23.

Second Kings 6:8 says that the king of Aram was at war with Israel. However, at this time it was not a full-scale war, but a series of border raids.

1. a. Why was the king of Aram angry? (2 Kings 6:8-11a)

    b. What did he do about the situation? (2 Kings 6:11b-14)

2. a. How did their situation appear to Elisha's servant? (2 Kings 6:15)

    b. What did Elisha ask God to reveal to the servant? (2 Kings 6:16-17)

3. Challenge: Although we may feel frightened and overwhelmed by our circumstances, what is the true situation for the person who has put their faith in Jesus Christ, according to the following verses?

    Romans 8:31

    1 John 4:4

4. How did God deliver Elisha and the people of Dothan from the forces of Aram? (2 Kings 6:18-20a) Locate Dothan and Samaria on the map on page 8.

5. a. In what situation did the soldiers of Aram find themselves when their eyes were opened? (2 Kings 6:20-21)

    b. How did Elisha intercede for the Arameans, and what was the final result? (2 Kings 6:22-23)

6. Personal: What threatening situation do you face today? Have you learned to see your circumstances from God's perspective instead of from a human perspective? If not, why not pray and ask God to help you trust in Him now? Read Psalm 34:4-7, and put your name in the verses if you would like to.

Third Day: Review 2 Kings 6:8—7:20, concentrating on 6:24-29.

1. a. God sent the temporary reprieve from war with Aram (see 2 Kings 6:23). From Romans 2:4, what do you learn about God's kindness?

    b. Apparently Israel did not repent of her sin, and God withdrew His protective hand.[1] What foreign army again threatened her? (2 Kings 6:24)

2. This time Ben-Hadad came with his entire army. What was the situation in Samaria because of the lengthy siege? (2 Kings 6:25)

3. When one of the Israelite women asked for the king's help, what fact did he acknowledge? (2 Kings 6:26-27)

4. a. Into what depth of depravity had some of the people fallen during the siege? (2 Kings 6:28-29)

    b. Read Leviticus 26:23-29. How did this incident in 2 Kings fulfill the prediction in Leviticus of what path Israel would take if she refused to repent of her sin?

5. Read Romans 1:18-21,28-32. If people refuse to follow God's way, what natural consequences follow?

---

1. *The Expositor's Bible Commentary.*

6. a. The Bible tells us that we are all sinners condemned to death (see Romans 3:23). Read Acts 20:21 and Romans 6:23. What hope are we given?

   b. Personal: Have you repented[1] and put your faith in Jesus Christ? If you haven't, won't you do it now? Remember, forgiveness and eternal life are free—they are gifts from God. If you have already repented, write briefly when this took place and what circumstances God used to bring you to that point.

Fourth Day: Review 2 Kings 6:8—7:20, concentrating on 6:30—7:2.

1. a. What was the king's reaction when he heard his subject's admission of cannibalism? (2 Kings 6:30a)

   b. What was he wearing under his royal robes? (2 Kings 6:30b)

   c. Challenge: Read Genesis 37:34 and 1 Kings 21:27-29a. In light of these passages, what might this king's actions in 2 Kings 6:30 have meant?

2. a. Although the king was grieving over the condition of his kingdom, in his anger and anguish whom did the he blame for Israel's circumstances? What did he vow to do? (2 Kings 6:31)

   b. The king sent a messenger to carry out his vow. Was this a surprise to Elisha? (2 Kings 6:32a)

   c. What did Elisha tell the elders to do, and why? (2 Kings 6:32b)

3. After making such a rash vow and sending the messenger to kill Elisha, the king rushed after the messenger and arrived at Elisha's house. Now, instead of blaming Elisha, whom did the king admit was responsible for the plight of his city? (2 Kings 6:33)

4. a. The restraint of the messenger and the king's words hint at the faint hope of God's intervention in this dire situation.[2] How did Elisha respond to the king's words? (2 Kings 7:1)

   b. Challenge: Compare the products for sale in 2 Kings 7:1 with those listed in 2 Kings 6:25. Was this an improvement?

---

1. The Hebrew word for "repent" means to change one's mind. (Dr. James Strong, The Exhaustive Concordance of the Bible, word number 3340)
2. *The Expositor's Bible Commentary.*

5. a. How did the king's officer react to Elisha's prediction? (2 Kings 7:2a)

    b. What judgment did Elisha pronounce on the officer's faithless unbelief? (2 Kings 7:2b)

6. Personal: God, in His providence, graciously promised through Elisha to bring an end to the siege and provide food for the people of Samaria. But the king's officer was not willing to believe that God could or would do such a thing. How do you respond to God's promises in the Bible? For example, read Revelation 21:1-7. When you consider how the world is today, how much evil seems to be in control, do you believe God can and will fulfill this promise?

Fifth Day: Review 2 Kings 6:8—7:20, concentrating on 7:3-11.

1. a. Where were the four men with leprosy? (2 Kings 7:3a)

    b. Challenge: Read Numbers 5:2-3. Why were these four men not allowed into the city?

2. What plan did the four men make? (2 Kings 7:3b-4)

3. What did they discover when they carried out their plan? (2 Kings 7:5)

4. How had God miraculously intervened for His people? (2 Kings 7:6-7)

5. After some time, what did the men realize they needed to do? (2 Kings 7:8-11)

6. Personal: Our God today is the same God who miraculously intervened for His people in this passage (see Malachi 3:6; Hebrews 13:8; and James 1:17). We may not necessarily see Him work in such spectacular ways, but He continues to hear and answer the prayers of His people. Do you look to Him in faith, trusting that He will guide you and protect you as you follow Him?

Sixth Day: Review 2 Kings 6:8—7:20, concentrating on 7:12-20.

1. The king had trouble believing that God had truly delivered them from the Arameans. What did he think might be the true situation? (2 Kings 7:12)

2. How did they find out what had really happened? (2 Kings 7:13-15)

3. How was Elisha's prophecy fulfilled? (2 Kings 7:16-20)

4. The officer's rejection of God's word given through Elisha brought divine judgment, resulting in his death. Yet God also, in His grace, delivered Israel from her enemies. Every person who has ever lived has sinned, and deserves death because of it (see Romans 3:23). In His grace, what way did God provide for any person who accepts it to be saved from death and receive eternal life? Read Romans 3:22-24 and 6:23.

5. Personal: Have you accepted God's gift of His Son, Jesus Christ, to cover your sin and save you from eternal death? Why not pray about this now?

2 Kings
Lesson 5

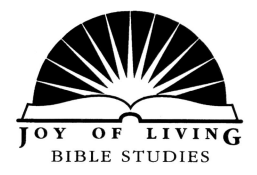

JOY OF LIVING
BIBLE STUDIES

2 Kings Chapters 6:8—7:20

Setting: The Northern Kingdom of Israel

Elisha not only ministered privately to individuals—as in our last lesson, to Naaman the Aramean commander and to the student prophets from the school at Jericho—but also served as God's prophet to the entire nation of Israel, playing a public role in the ongoing conflict between Aram and Israel. Second Kings 6:8 says that the king of Aram was at war with Israel. However, at this time it was not a full-scale war, but a series of border raids.

The king of Aram tried again and again to ambush the Israelites, but each time Elisha warned the king of Israel where the Arameans were camped, so the Israelites were on guard and could not be taken by surprise. The king of Aram was furious, and he accused his officers of harboring a traitor who had been giving away their position to Israel. Elisha's aid to the Israelite king had apparently become common knowledge, so one of the Aramean officers reported to his king that it was Elisha the prophet who was reporting their private conversations to the king of Israel: "the very words you speak in your bedroom" (2 Kings 6:12).

What a great reminder of the reality of God's omniscience—He knows everything about everyone at all times. As Psalm 139:1-4 says, "You have searched me, Lord, and you know me. You know when I sit and when I rise; you perceive my thoughts from afar. You discern my going out and my lying down; you are familiar with all my ways. Before a word is on my tongue you, Lord, know it completely." If we think we are hiding some activity, thought, or attitude from Him, we should think again. On the other hand, it is wonderful to know that God knows all about us—even our thoughts—and He still loves us and cares about us.

The king of Aram decided to send men to capture Elisha. Discovering that Elisha was in Dothan, the king sent a strong force by night and surrounded the city. Dothan was located on a hill about halfway between Jezreel and Samaria, where the main royal residences of Israel were.[1] It was only about 11 miles north of Samaria,[2] the capital city, where presumably the army of Israel was centered. The fact that Aram could send its force so close to the capital says much about Israel's military weakness and Aram's strength at this time.

God's Power Unveiled

The next morning, Elisha's servant went out and saw the Aramean army surrounding the city. Frightened, he reported this to Elisha, but Elisha was not alarmed. He knew that God's unseen forces were far stronger than this visible human army. Elisha prayed that God would open his servant's eyes. Then, the servant looked "and saw the hills full of horses and chariots of fire" (2 Kings 6:17)—God's angelic host. Psalm 34:7 assures us, "The angel of the Lord encamps around those who fear him, and he delivers them." We may not be able to see God's forces with our eyes as Elisha's servant did, but we can see them with eyes of faith and trust that God will deliver us.

As the enemy soldiers came toward Elisha to capture him, he prayed that the Lord would strike them with blindness, and God did as he asked. Elisha then told them, "This is not the road and this is not the city. Follow me, and I will lead you to the man you are looking for" (2 Kings 6:19). They evidently believed him, because they followed him. They were about to 'find Elisha,' but not quite in the manner they had planned. Elisha led them to the city of Samaria, and there asked God to open their eyes once again. How horrified they must have been to find themselves inside the fortress-like capital city of their enemy. They intended to be captors of Elisha, but instead they were captives.

The king of Israel was ready to kill the Arameans, but Elisha intervened and instructed the king to feed them and send them back to their master. Afterward, recognizing the futility of opposition to the power of the God of Israel, the bands from Aram stopped raiding Israel's territory, at least temporarily.

The physical eyes of Elisha's servant were opened in order for him to see and recognize God's mighty power. The physical eyes of the Aramean soldiers were blinded and later opened again in order for them to see and recognize God's mighty power.

God still opens people's eyes today. Jesus died and rose again so that we can be forgiven, have a relationship with God, and "see" His truth and glory. God sent the Apostle Paul to the Gentiles "to open their eyes and turn them from darkness to light, and from the power of Satan to God, so that they may receive forgiveness of sins and a place among those who are sanctified by faith in me [Jesus Christ]"(Acts 26:18). Only when God opens our spiritual eyes can we see His truth and turn to Him for forgiveness.

1. *NIV Study Notes* on 2 Kings 6:13.
2. Ibid, note on 2 Kings 6:8.

Paul tells us, "The god of this age [Satan] has blinded the minds of unbelievers, so that they cannot see the light of the gospel that displays the glory of Christ, who is the image of God. For what we preach is not ourselves, but Jesus Christ as Lord...For God, who said, 'Let light shine out of darkness,' made his light shine in our hearts to give us the light of the knowledge of God's glory displayed in the face of Christ" (2 Corinthians 4:4-6.)

God has chosen to use the "foolishness" of preaching so that people can be saved (1 Corinthians 1:21; see also Romans 10:12-17). This salvation is more than just having our sins forgiven. It includes:

- being born of God's Spirit (see 1 Peter 1:23)

- being justified (see Romans 3:24)

- being reconciled to God (see Colossians 1:22)

- being able to see and understand His truth and glory (see 1 Corinthians 2:6-16; 2 Corinthians 4:6; Ephesians 1:18-19a).

In 2 Kings, God used Elisha so that people could see and recognize God's mighty power. Today, sharing God's truth is the responsibility of every person who has been born again by God's Spirit (see 2 Timothy 4:2).

You may not feel capable of this, but 1 Peter 3:15 says, "Always be prepared to give an answer to everyone who asks you to give the reason for the hope that you have." You may not be able to preach a sermon, but you can share what God has done for you. Romans 10:13-14 tells us, "Everyone who calls on the name of the Lord will be saved. How, then, can they call on the one they have not believed in? And how can they believe in the one of whom they have not heard?" If you don't share God's truth with them, who will?

God's Protection Withdrawn

God may have sent the temporary reprieve from war with Aram to remind Israel of His love and concern for His people. But apparently Israel did not repent of her sin, and God withdrew His protective hand. Israel now faced an invasion by the entire army of Aram, led by Ben-Hadad, the king of Aram, himself. The Arameans marched all the way to the capital city of Samaria and laid siege to it. The siege lasted so long that the population was starving. Even the most unlikely commodities—a donkey's head, seed pods—went for hugely inflated prices.

One day, as the king of Israel walked by on the wall of the city, a woman called out for his help. The king's reply showed that he recognized his own inability to help her if the Lord did not once again act on Israel's behalf. However, he also implied that the whole situation was God's fault, rather than a situation brought about by Israel's disobedience and idolatry.

The woman's story showed how depraved the people had become. She had made an arrangement with another woman that one day they would kill, cook, and eat her own son, and the next day they would cook the other woman's son—but after the first day, the second woman hid her son. Cannibalism! The sins of Israel's king and people

were so great that the covenant curses found in Leviticus and Deuteronomy were now being inflicted upon them:

- "If in spite of this you still do not listen to me but continue to be hostile toward me, then in my anger I will be hostile toward you, and I myself will punish you for your sins seven times over. You will eat the flesh of your sons and the flesh of your daughters." (Leviticus 26:27-29)

- "They will lay siege to all the cities throughout your land until the high fortified walls in which you trust fall down. They will besiege all the cities throughout the land the Lord your God is giving you. Because of the suffering that your enemy will inflict on you during the siege, you will eat the fruit of the womb, the flesh of the sons and daughters the Lord your God has given you." (Deuteronomy 28:52-53)

When people refuse to follow God's way, He allows the natural consequences of their sinfulness to take effect. As the Apostle Paul explained in Romans 1:21,28-29, "For although they knew God, they neither glorified him as God nor gave thanks to him, but their thinking became futile and their foolish hearts were darkened...Furthermore, just as they did not think it worthwhile to retain the knowledge of God, so God gave them over to a depraved mind, so that they do what ought not to be done. They have become filled with every kind of wickedness, evil, greed and depravity."

The king of Israel was horrified at the woman's words, and he tore his royal robes, revealing that he was wearing sackcloth garments underneath. Sackcloth was a coarse cloth usually worn as a sign of mourning or repentance. However, as the king immediately declared that he would behead Elisha, we see that his sackcloth didn't indicate repentance and sorrow for sin, but rather was an expression of mourning over Israel's situation coupled with anger toward Elisha and the Lord.

In the meantime, Elisha was sitting in his house, and the elders, or leaders, of the city were sitting with him. By God's power, Elisha knew that the king had sent someone to behead him. He instructed the elders to keep the door closed against the messenger, as Elisha knew the king would immediately follow. When the king arrived, he said, "This disaster is from the Lord. Why should I wait for the Lord any longer?" (2 Kings 6:33). The king realized that his situation was from the Lord and had all but given up hope of the Lord's deliverance.

But Elisha, and the Lord, surprised him. Elisha prophesied, "This is what the Lord says: About this time tomorrow, a seah of the finest flour will sell for a shekel and two seahs of barley for a shekel at the gate of Samaria" (2 Kings 7:1). Good food products would be available again by the next day. The prices would still be about double the normal cost, but still a wonderful improvement.

The king's chief aide expressed his skepticism with ridicule and sarcasm, "Look, even if the Lord should open the floodgates of the heavens, could this happen?" (2 Kings 7:2). Elisha assured him that the prophecy would come to pass, and that the officer would see it with his own eyes, but he would not eat any of it. Due to his disbelief, he would miss out on God's blessing on the people of Israel.

The Siege Is Lifted

In 2 Kings 7:3, the scene changes to a group of four men with leprosy outside the entrance to the city. According to the Law of Moses, anyone who had "a defiling skin disease" was to be sent "outside the camp" so they would not defile the people (Numbers 5:2-3). Though these men were apparently unmolested by the besieging Arameans, their situation was desperate—they were trapped between the famine in the city and their own lack of food sources outside the gates. They decided to go surrender to the Arameans, and either be killed or be spared. It seemed to them better than slow starvation.

At dusk, they went to the Aramean camp, and to their surprise, no one was there! The Arameans had abandoned their tents and furnishings, along with their horses and donkeys, in a panicked flight. The Lord had caused them to hear what seemed to them to be the approach of a great army to liberate the besieged Israelites—perhaps, they thought, an army of Hittites and Egyptians.

The four lepers entered various tents, eating and drinking their fill, taking valuables and going off to hide them. But then they realized that it was their duty to tell the good news to the besieged Israelites—not to mention, if they waited too long to tell, they might receive God's punishment. So they went back to the city gates and told the gatekeepers, who passed the news along until it finally reached the palace.

Sometimes we tend to forget that failing to do what is right is just as sinful as doing what is wrong. We may push to the back of our mind the prompting of the Holy Spirit to take action and make excuses for ourselves. However, James 4:17 says, "If anyone, then, knows the good they ought to do and doesn't do it, it is sin for them." Pause for just a moment and ask God to show you in what way, if any, you may have failed to do what He has prompted you to do. Ask His forgiveness, and as soon as possible act in obedience.

The king had trouble believing that the Arameans had really left. Maybe they had only withdrawn temporarily to tempt the Israelites to leave the protection of the city walls. On the advice of his officers, he sent some of his men with two chariots and horses to discover the truth. These scouts returned and confirmed the amazing news that the Arameans had indeed fled in panic, leaving clothing and equipment all along the road as far as the Jordan River.

At this news, the people were allowed out the city gate, where they plundered the Aramean camp. The king had put his chief aide in charge of the gate, and as the people madly rushed out the gate, they trampled the officer to death, thus fulfilling Elisha's prophecy regarding him, "You will see it with your own eyes, but you will not eat any of it!" (2 Kings 7:19). Every aspect of God's prophetic word spoken by Elisha was shown to be trustworthy:

- Israel was reminded that her deliverance from her enemy was a gift of God's grace.

- The officer's death demonstrated that rejection of God's Word leads to divine judgment.

Like the Israelites, we each face the choice of whether we will believe God's Word or not. We may not face immediate death for our unbelief, as the unbelieving Israelite officer did, but it is surely coming. As Romans 6:23 says, "For the wages of sin is death, but the gift of God is eternal life in Christ Jesus our Lord." Have you decided whether to believe God and accept his gift of salvation? (See page 4 for more information.)

Study Questions

Before you begin your study this week:
- ❧ Pray and ask God to speak to you through His Holy Spirit.
- ❧ Use only the Bible for your answers.
- ❧ Write down your answers and the verses you used.
- ❧ Answer the "Challenge" questions if you have the time and want to do them.
- ❧ Share your answers to the "Personal" questions with the class only if you want to share them.

First Day: Read the Commentary on 2 Kings 6:8—7:20.

1. What meaningful or new thought did you find in the Commentary on 2 Kings 6:8—7:20 or from your teacher's lecture?

2. Look for a verse in the lesson to memorize this week. Write it down, carry it with you, or post it in a prominent place. Make a real effort to learn the verse and its "address" (reference of where it is found in the Bible).

Second Day: Read 2 Kings 8-10, concentrating on 8:1-15.

1. a. We again meet the devout Shunammite woman whose story was told in 2 Kings chapter 4. What did Elisha warn her about in 2 Kings 8:1?

   b. What problem did she encounter when she and her family returned to Israel, and what did she do about it? (2 Kings 8:2-3)

2. Who was with the king at this time, and how did his testimony aid the woman's case?[1] (2 Kings 8:4-6)

3. Personal: Some people would say the woman was "lucky" that Gehazi just "happened" to be there when she went before the king. We, however, know that God is in control of all the circumstances of our lives (see Psalm 139; Proverbs 16:9). In this incident we see again how God, providentially, provided for and blessed those who were obedient to His Word given through His prophets. If you are a Christian, do you desire to walk in His ways, and trust that He will provide for you and bless you? Read Matthew 6:31-33 and Romans 15:13, and write down your thoughts about this.

4. Review 1 Kings 19:15-16. What had the Lord instructed the prophet Elijah to do? The task of anointing these two kings was passed along to Elijah's successor, Elisha, to actually carry out, as we will see in 2 Kings 8 and 9.

5. a. How did Elisha carry out the first task God had given to Elijah in 1 Kings 19:15, and why did it cause him to weep? (2 Kings 8:7-13)

---

1. *The Expositor's Bible Commentary* notes, "The time of the encounter has been much debated, many suggesting that the meeting must have taken place before Gehazi had contracted leprosy...If the text is in chronological order, one may have reason to conjecture that Gehazi had repented of his sins and had been restored to a place of usefulness for God, despite his forfeiture of position with Elisha."

b. Elisha told Hazael to inform Ben-Hadad that he would recover—that his illness was not terminal. How did Ben-Hadad actually die? (2 Kings 8:14-15)

6. Personal: Elisha wept because the Lord had revealed to him the severity of the judgment He was about to send upon Israel by the hand of Hazael.[1] God has revealed to us in His Word the judgment that Jesus Christ will carry out when He returns to earth (see Matthew 25:31-46). Do you weep for those who have not believed in Jesus Christ and therefore will be punished by eternal separation from God? Whom do you need to tell about Jesus' gracious gift of salvation?

Third Day: Review 2 Kings 8-10, concentrating on 8:16-24.

1. The author of Kings now returns his attention to the kings of Judah, the southern kingdom. How old was Jehoram when he became king, and how long did he reign? (2 Kings 8:16-17)

2. a. How was Jehoram's spiritual leadership characterized? What evil influence did he have in his life? (2 Kings 8:18)

   b. Challenge: Read 1 Kings 16:30-33 to see what evil Ahab had done, that Jehoram now imitated.

3. a. Why did God spare Judah and its royal house the judgment that He had brought on the house of Ahab? (2 Kings 8:19)

   b. Challenge: Read God's original promise to David in 2 Samuel 7:16; then read 1 Kings 11:34-36 to see how He began to fulfill this promise in David's son Solomon's time, when the kingdom was divided.

4. Although God honored His covenant with David and did not destroy Judah during Jehoram's reign, Jehoram and Judah did experience judgment in the form of military defeats.[2] What countries rebelled against Judah during Jehoram's reign? (2 Kings 8:20-22)

5. Challenge: The writer of Chronicles wrote about additional divine judgments brought against Jehoram. What else happened in 2 Chronicles 21:16-19?

---

1. *The NIV Study Bible.*
2. *The Expositor's Bible Commentary.*

6. Personal: Jehoram probably thought he "had it made" and could do whatever he wanted with no consequences. How about you? Perhaps you accepted Christ a long time ago, and now you think you can do whatever you want, with no consequences, because you're "saved." What do you learn from Galatians 6:7 and Colossians 3:24b-25?

Fourth Day: Review 2 Kings 8-10, concentrating on 8:25-29.

1. Who succeeded Jehoram on the throne of Judah? (2 Kings 8:25)

2. How old was he and how long did he reign? (2 Kings 8:26)

3. a. What was his spiritual character? (2 Kings 8:27)

   b. Challenge: Read 1 Kings 22:41-43 and review 2 Kings 8:16-18. Also read 2 Chronicles 22:3-4, which is a parallel passage about Ahaziah. Compare the spiritual characteristics of Jehoshaphat, his son Jehoram, and his grandson Ahaziah. From 2 Kings 8:18,26b-27 and 2 Chronicles 22:3-4, who was the chief influence on both Jehoram and Ahaziah to do evil?

4. What relationship did Ahaziah king of Judah maintain with the king of Israel? (2 Kings 8:28-29)

5. Read Deuteronomy 7:1-4 and 2 Corinthians 6:14-17. Why did God instruct believers in both Old and New Testament times not to marry unbelievers?

6. Personal: Even though Athaliah was an Israelite, she did not serve the Lord, and she turned both her husband and son away from the Lord. What outcomes have you witnessed in marriages between a believer and an unbeliever? If a believer came to you for counsel before marrying an unbeliever, what would you tell them?

Fifth Day: Review 2 Kings 8-10, concentrating on chapter 9.

1. What did Elisha instruct one of the prophets to do? (2 Kings 9:1-3)

2. a. What did the prophet tell Jehu that God would use him to accomplish? (2 Kings 9:7-10)

    b. Challenge: Read 1 Kings 21:20-29. Why wasn't this judgment carried out during Ahab's lifetime? (verses 28-29)

3. a. How did Jehu begin to carry out his commission to "destroy the house of Ahab"? (2 Kings 9:11-24; summarize briefly)

    b. How was Ahab and Jezebel's murder of Naboth finally avenged? (2 Kings 9:25-26; see also 1 Kings 21:1-19)

4. a. What happened to King Ahaziah of Judah? (2 Kings 9:27-28)

    b. Challenge: Read 2 Chronicles 22:7a. Why did Ahaziah die?

5. How did Jehu carry out God's judgment upon Ahab's widow, Jezebel? (2 Kings 9:30-37; summarize briefly)

6. Personal: God's judgment of the evil of Ahab and Jezebel was finally carried out. But people continue to do evil, and often it seems as if they get away with it. Read 2 Peter 3:8-13. How does this help you understand God's "delay" in dealing with evil in the world? Are you encouraged to live a holy and godly life as you look forward to His coming?

Sixth Day: Review 2 Kings 8-10, concentrating on chapter 10.

1. a. Although Jehu had killed Ahab's son Jehoram and wife Jezebel, he had not completed his commission to "destroy the house of Ahab… cut off from Ahab every last male" (2 Kings 9:7-8). How did he further fulfill the commission? (2 Kings 10:1-11b, summarize briefly)

b. Who else did Jehu execute, ensuring there would be no one who might attempt to continue Ahab's ungodly reign? (2 Kings 10:11b-14)

2. a. Whom did Jehu meet and invite to join him? (2 Kings 10:15-16)

    b. Challenge: What does Jeremiah 35:6-10 tell us about the Recabites?

3. How did Jehu complete the commission to destroy the house of Ahab? (2 Kings 10:17)

4. Along with bringing judgment to the house of Ahab, Jehu acted to purge Israel of Baal worship. How did he accomplish this in 2 Kings 10:18-29? (Summarize briefly.)

5. a. What did God commend Jehu for? (2 Kings 10:30)

    b. How did Jehu fall short of God's desire for Him, and what was the result? (2 Kings 10:31-33)

    c. How long did Jehu rule over Israel? (2 Kings 10:36)

6. Personal: Jehu began his service as Israel's new king by fulfilling God's commission to destroy the house of Ahab. He destroyed the worship of Baal, but continued to worship the golden calves established by Jeroboam. The problem was, he "was not careful to keep the law...*with all his heart*" (2 Kings 10:31, italics added). In the same way, we might do good things and obey what God says in some areas of our life, but also do selfish and sinful things because we haven't made Him Lord of our lives. Do you want to serve the Lord with all your heart? Why not pray about this now?

2 Kings
Lesson 6

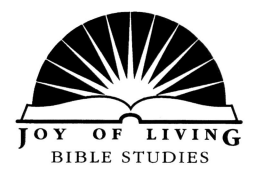

JOY OF LIVING
BIBLE STUDIES

2 Kings Chapters 8-10

Setting: The Northern Kingdom of Israel

Do you remember the woman from Shunem that we met in 2 Kings chapter 4? The prophet Elisha had often stopped at her house to eat and rest. She and her husband had made and furnished a small room on their roof for Elisha to stay in whenever he came to their town. Elisha had wondered what he might do to repay her kindness. After his servant pointed out that the woman was childless and that her husband was old, Elisha promised the woman, "About this time next year...you will hold a son in your arms" (2 Kings 4:16). The child was born and grew, but one day, out in the fields with his father, he became suddenly and critically ill, and he died in his mother's arms the same day. When Elisha prayed for the boy, the Lord had restored him to life.

Some time later, Elisha had warned the woman, "Go away with your family and stay for a while wherever you can, because the Lord has decreed a famine in the land that will last seven years" (2 Kings 8:1). She followed Elisha's instructions, and, she and her family went to the land of the Philistines for seven years. While she was away, either someone had illegally occupied her property, or else it was considered to be abandoned and therefore fell under the king's control.

As chapter 8 begins, this Shunammite woman went to appeal to the king for the return of her house and land. Since there is no mention of her husband, it appears that by this time he had died and she was a widow.

At that very moment, the king was talking to Elisha's former servant, Gehazi.[1] This meeting of the king, Gehazi, and the woman was not a mere coincidence. God had arranged their encounter so that Gehazi could identify the woman to the king, thereby helping to verify her claim to her land. In addition, the woman was living proof for the king of God's mighty miracles accomplished through the prophet Elisha. The king believed the woman's story. He assigned an official to her case and instructed him to give back everything that belonged to

her, including all the income from her land that had accrued during the time she was out of the country.

Just as God controlled events in that day, providing for and blessing those who were obedient to His Word given through His prophets, so He will provide for and bless obedient believers today. Romans 8:28 promises, "And we know that in all things God works for the good of those who love him, who have been called according to his purpose." Do you love Him and desire to walk in His ways? Are you trusting in Him to provide for and bless you? In Matthew 6:31-33 He reminds us, "Do not worry, saying, 'What shall we eat?' or 'What shall we drink?' or 'What shall we wear?' For the pagans run after all these things, and your heavenly Father knows that you need them. But seek first his kingdom and his righteousness, and all these things will be given to you as well."

The Anointing of Hazael

Back in 1 Kings 19:15-16, prior to being taken to heaven in a whirlwind, the prophet Elijah had been instructed by the Lord to anoint Hazael king over Aram and Jehu son of Nimshi king over Israel. These tasks were passed along to Elijah's successor, Elisha.

Now, in 2 Kings 8, the time had come for Elisha to carry out the first anointing. He traveled to Damascus, the capital city of Aram. At this time, King Ben-Hadad of Aram was ill, and when he heard the prophet was in the city, he asked Hazael, one of his trusted officials, to "Consult the Lord through him" (2 Kings 8:8). Surprisingly, this pagan king was seeking a message from Israel's God.

Hazael was to take a gift to Elisha and ask him if Ben-Hadad would recover from his illness. This gift was not just a small token of esteem—Hazael took forty camel-loads of all the finest wares of Damascus. Perhaps Ben-Hadad thought such a large gift would cause Elisha to give him a favorable message from the Lord. The Bible doesn't tell us how Elisha responded to Ben-Hadad's gift, but remember that he refused to accept anything from the Aramean commander, Naaman, who had come to him for healing from leprosy (see 2 Kings 5:16).

Hazael obeyed his master's instructions. When Elisha heard Ben-Hadad's question, "Will I recover from this illness?" he answered Hazael, "Go and say to him, 'You will certainly recover.' Nevertheless, the Lord has revealed to me that he will in fact die" (2 Kings 8:9-10). The verbal assurance of recovery was true—Ben-Hadad's illness was

---

1. Remember, in 2 Kings 5, after Gehazi's greed led him to take Naaman's gifts for himself and hide them from Elisha, Elisha announced Gehazi's punishment—he and his descendants would suffer from the leprosy from which Naaman had been healed, and Gehazi was banished in disgrace from Elisha's presence. Some Bible commentators suggest that this meeting must have taken place before Gehazi contracted leprosy. Others say that Gehazi may have repented of his sins and been restored to a place of usefulness for God, despite forfeiting his position with Elisha. (*The Expositor's Bible Commentary*, notes on 2 Kings 8:1-6.)

not terminal. However, Elisha knew that Hazael would plot the king's death, and carry out a coup d'etat. Elisha stared at Hazael until Hazael was embarrassed.

Then Elisha began to weep. When Hazael asked why, Elisha answered that he knew what terrible things Hazael would inflict on the northern kingdom of Israel. Hazael wondered how he could gain the power to accomplish such things. Then Elisha spoke the words, "The Lord has shown me that you will become king of Aram" (2 Kings 8:13). As he spoke these words to Hazael, Elisha was, in effect, anointing him king of Aram.

So Hazael returned to his master and told him that Elisha said he would surely recover. But the next day Hazael smothered Ben-Hadad and assumed the throne of Aram.

As Elisha had foretold, Aram would carry out the judgment the Lord would send upon His disobedient people. Elisha's foreknowledge did not authorize or approve of the atrocities to be carried out by the Arameans, but simply described future events.

This was not God's desire for Israel. As He said in Ezekiel 33:11, "As surely as I live, declares the Sovereign LORD, I take no pleasure in the death of the wicked, but rather that they turn from their ways and live. Turn! Turn from your evil ways! Why will you die, people of Israel?"

God's Word says that Jesus Christ will carry out God's judgment of unbelievers when He returns to earth (see Matthew 25:31-46). Those who have not accepted His gift of salvation will suffer eternal separation from God. This is not God's desire, either. He has gone to such great lengths to provide the way of forgiveness for those who will just accept His gift.

As a believer, do you weep as Elisha did when you consider this future judgment of unbelievers? Does this knowledge spur you on to tell others about Jesus' gift of salvation, freely available to anyone who will accept it?

King Jehoram of Judah

Setting: The Southern Kingdom of Judah

In 2 Kings 8:17, the author now turns his attention from the northern kingdom of Israel and its enemy, Aram, to the southern kingdom of Judah. Jehoram of Judah began his reign at the age of 32, and ruled for 8 years. The evaluation of his reign was, "He did evil in the eyes of the Lord" (2 Kings 8:18). Second Chronicles 21:11 adds, "He had also built high places on the hills of Judah and had caused the people of Jerusalem to prostitute themselves and had led Judah astray."

Jehoram's father, King Jehoshaphat, had been a godly ruler, but Jehoram married Athaliah, a daughter of King Ahab of Israel. Ahab "did more to arouse the anger of the Lord, the God of Israel, than did all the kings of Israel before him" (1 Kings 16:33). Athaliah, a wicked woman (see 2 Chronicles 24:7), influenced Jehoram to follow the ways of her father, Ahab. After Jehoshaphat's death, Jehoram killed all of his brothers (see 2 Chronicles 21:4). In spite of Jehoram's evil

actions, God honored His covenant with the house of David and did not yet send a final judgment of destruction upon Judah (see 2 Samuel 7:16; 1 Kings 11:34-36; 2 Kings 8:19).

However, Jehoram did experience judgment from the Lord. 2 Chronicles 21 says he received a letter from the prophet Elijah, which warned him that because of his evil ways the Lord was "about to strike your people, your sons, your wives and everything that is yours, with a heavy blow. You yourself will be very ill with a lingering disease of the bowels, until the disease causes your bowels to come out" (2 Chronicles 21:14-15). Jehoram also suffered several military defeats:

> ஜ Edom, which had been subject to Judah, rebelled and set up its own king. Jehoram tried to suppress the rebellion, but failed (see 2 Kings 8:20-22).

> ஜ Libnah also revolted (see 2 Kings 8:22).

> ஜ The Philistines and the Arabs who lived near the Cushites invaded Judah and carried off all the goods from the king's palace, along with all his sons and wives. Only the youngest son, Ahaziah, was left to him (see 2 Chronicles 21:16-17).

And finally, "The Lord afflicted Jehoram with an incurable disease of the bowels. In the course of time, at the end of the second year, his bowels came out because of the disease, and he died in great pain" (2 Chronicles 21:18-19).

Jehoram had probably heard of God's covenant with his forefather, David. He probably witnessed his father Jehoshaphat's worship of the Lord at the temple in Jerusalem. But somehow, it didn't mean anything to him, and he worshiped pagan gods with his wife Athaliah. In spite of Elijah's letter warning him of God's coming judgments, Jehoram didn't repent. God fulfilled His Word and carried out the judgments. Have you or someone you know been ignoring the warnings of judgment in God's Word? (See Galatians 6:7; Ephesians 5:5-6.) If you need more information on how to repent and turn to Him for forgiveness, see page 4.

King Ahaziah of Judah

Ahaziah, son of Jehoram, succeeded to the throne of Judah when his father died. He was only twenty-two years old, and he reigned only one year. Second Kings 8:27 says, "He followed the ways of the house of Ahab and did evil in the eyes of the Lord, as the house of Ahab had done, for he was related by marriage to Ahab's family." His mother, Athaliah, influenced him for evil, just as she had influenced her husband, Jehoram.

King Ahaziah of Judah joined his uncle, King Joram of Israel, to fight against Israel's enemy, Hazael king of Aram, at Ramoth Gilead, a city in the northern part of Israel. When Joram was wounded in battle, he returned to Jezreel to recover, and Ahaziah went to visit him there. As we will see in the next chapter, this would prove to be Ahaziah's undoing.

In the lives of both Jehoram and Ahaziah, we see the terrible influence for evil that the unbelieving Athaliah brought to Judah when she married Jehoram. In both the Old and New Testaments, God instructed His people not to marry unbelievers (see Deuteronomy 7:4; 2 Corinthians 6:14). His guidelines are as important for us today as they were for Israel in the Promised Land. A person may think they will be able to maintain their own faith even when married to an unbeliever, but the very fact that they chose to be disobedient to the Lord's instructions shows that they have already begun to compromise their faith, and they may be sadly surprised at how much more their spouse's unbelief will pull them away from the Lord.

Jehu Anointed King of Israel

Setting: The Northern Kingdom of Israel

The time had come for Elisha to carry out the second anointing that the Lord had originally assigned to the prophet Elijah, a task that was passed along to Elisha as his successor (see 1 Kings 19:15-16). Elisha summoned a man from the company of the prophets and sent him to Ramoth Gilead with instructions to anoint Jehu, the commander of Israel's army, as the next king of Israel. After carrying out his task, the prophet was to leave Jehu immediately and run away.

The prophet instructed Jehu to destroy King Ahab's entire "house," including his wife, Jezebel, in order to avenge the blood of God's prophets who had been martyred for their faithfulness. King Ahab had already died, and his son Joram was now king. The Lord's judgment against Ahab and his house had been delayed until after his death because Ahab had finally humbled himself before the Lord (see 1 Kings 21:28-29).

When Jehu told his fellow officers what the prophet had said, they enthusiastically celebrated his anointing. Their current king, Joram, was in Jezreel, recovering from battle wounds. Jehu charged his officers to keep everyone in Ramoth Gilead so the news of his anointing wouldn't reach Joram in Jezreel. Then he took his chariot and a select group of troops and rode to Jezreel, which was about forty-five miles away.

When Jehu arrived, Joram and King Ahaziah of Judah, who was visiting Joram, each rode his own chariot out to meet Jehu. They all met at the plot of ground that had belonged to Naboth, whom Ahab's wife Jezebel had murdered because Ahab wanted his property (see 1 Kings 21:1-14). Joram asked Jehu, "Have you come in peace?" Jehu answered, "How can there be peace...as long as all the idolatry and witchcraft of your mother Jezebel abound?" (2 Kings 9:22).

Joram immediately warned Ahaziah of treachery and turned to flee, but was killed by Jehu's arrow. Jehu saw this as the fulfillment of Elijah's prophecy against Ahab (see 1 Kings 21:19) in payment for the blood of Naboth: "Jehu said to Bidkar, his chariot officer, 'Pick him up and throw him on the field that belonged to Naboth the Jezreelite. Remember how you and I were riding together in chariots behind Ahab his father when the Lord spoke this prophecy against him: "Yesterday I saw the blood of Naboth and the blood of his sons, declares the Lord, and I will surely make you pay for it on this plot of ground, declares the Lord." Now then, pick him up and throw him on that plot, in accordance with the word of the Lord'" (2 Kings 9:25-26).

Jehu then chased King Ahaziah of Judah and wounded him, but Ahaziah escaped to Megiddo before dying of his injuries. This, too, was part of God's judgment: "Through Ahaziah's visit to Joram, God brought about Ahaziah's downfall" (2 Chronicles 22:7).

Next, Jehu carried out God's judgment on Ahab's widow, Jezebel. Entering Jezreel, he found her at an upper window of the palace, and she taunted him as "you murderer of your master" (2 Kings 9:31). Jehu told some of her servants to throw her out the window, and she fell to her death. He rode over her fallen body and went inside to dine in the palace of the king. After a while, he gave instructions to bury Jezebel, since she was a king's daughter, but when they went out, there was nothing left but her skull, her feet, and her hands. Jehu realized that this fulfilled Elijah's prophecy: "And also concerning Jezebel the Lord says: 'Dogs will devour Jezebel by the wall of Jezreel.'" (1 Kings 21:23).

God's judgment of the evil of Ahab and Jezebel was finally carried out. Today, people continue to do evil, and sometimes it seems as if they get away with it. The apostle Peter wrote, "With the Lord a day is like a thousand years, and a thousand years are like a day. The Lord is not slow in keeping his promise, as some understand slowness. Instead he is patient with you, not wanting anyone to perish, but everyone to come to repentance. But the day of the Lord will come like a thief. The heavens will disappear with a roar; the elements will be destroyed by fire, and the earth and everything done in it will be laid bare" (2 Peter 3:8-10). So, in the long run, no one will "get away" with sin. They will be subject to God's judgment at "the day of the Lord." In the meantime, won't you encourage everyone you know to repent and trust in Jesus Christ for forgiveness, so they won't have to suffer God's judgment?

Ahab's House Is Destroyed

As we read earlier, the prophet who anointed Jehu instructed him, "You are to destroy the house of Ahab your master" (2 Kings 9:7). This meant all the members of the royal family were to be eliminated. Jehu wrote to the elders and guardians of Ahab's children in Samaria, "If you are on my side and will obey me, take the heads of your master's sons and come to me in Jezreel by this time tomorrow" (2 Kings 10:6). The guardians slaughtered all 70 princes and sent their heads in baskets to Jehu. Jehu then declared, "Know, then, that not a word the Lord has spoken against the house of Ahab will fail. The Lord has done what he announced through his servant Elijah" (2 Kings 10:10).

Jehu killed all of Ahab's "chief men, his close friends, and his priests, leaving him no survivor" (2 Kings 10:11). Then, meeting 42 relatives of King Ahaziah of Judah, who were traveling to visit the royal family of Samaria, he killed them as well. Since the two royal houses of Israel and Judah were related, Jehu wanted to make sure that no one with a possible claim to Ahab's throne survived.

As Jehu traveled on, he met Jehonadab son of Rekab, who was on his way to meet him. The prophet Jeremiah later wrote that Jehonadab was the leader of a group that lived a nomadic life in the desert, drinking no wine, living in tents, and sowing no crops (see Jeremiah 35:6-10). They lived in protest to the materialism and religious compromise in Israel. Perhaps Jehonadab hoped that under this new king Israel would repent and return to the Lord.[1] When Jehu asked him if he was in agreement with him, Jehonadab said that he was, and Jehu invited him to ride along in his chariot to witness Jehu's further zeal for the Lord. When Jehu reached the city of Samaria, he killed all who remained there of Ahab's family, carrying out the remainder of God's judgment again the house of Ahab.

As you read this you may feel that God's judgment was harsh, but consider this. If a person has cancer, every cancer cell must be destroyed; otherwise that cell will begin to multiply and spread all over again. The house of Ahab was totally corrupt. They had led the entire kingdom of Israel into the pagan worship of Baal and other false gods. Countless people will spend eternity separated from God because of the evil influence of Ahab and his family. God knew that if Ahab's family had continued, they would have again led countless souls to hell. It was God's love as well as His justice that issued such judgment.

Baal Worship Destroyed in Israel

Now Jehu came up with a deceptive plan to purge Israel of Baal worship. He pretended that he himself wanted to worship Baal, and summoned all the prophets, servants, and priests of Baal to come to a great sacrifice to Baal. Whoever didn't show up would be killed, so they all came. When they had all crowded into the temple of Baal, each Baal worshipper was given a special robe, making them easier to identify.

Jehu had posted eighty men outside, warning them to keep anyone from escaping, or they themselves would die. After he finished making the burnt offering, he sent in his guards and officers to kill all the worshippers of Baal. After all were killed, they entered the inner shrine of Baal, brought out the sacred stone and burned it, and then tore down the temple, turning it over to the people to use as a latrine.

Jehu's Shortcomings

The Lord commended Jehu, "You have done well in accomplishing what is right in my eyes and have done to the house of Ahab all I had in mind to do" (2 Kings 10:30). However, Jehu "did not turn away from the sins of Jeroboam son of Nebat, which he had caused Israel to commit—the worship of the golden calves at Bethel and Dan...[He] was not careful to keep the law of the Lord, the God of Israel, with all his heart" (2 Kings 10:29,31). As a result, the Lord began to reduce the size of Israel by allowing King Hazael of Aram to seize some of Israel's land.

Jehu reigned over Israel for 28 years. Though some, such as Jehonadab, may have hoped for Israel to turn to the Lord wholeheart-

edly under Jehu's reign, they were disappointed. Today, we too may hope that some human leader will restore our church, our community, or our nation to truly follow the Lord. It is not wrong to hope this and work towards it, but any human leader is bound to disappoint us in the long run. People, even Christian believers, are still sinful and fallible. We can't put our ultimate trust in them, nor will anything be perfect until our Lord returns.

The entire Old Testament continually pointed forward to the Messiah, who would come to save His people and to save all humanity. In the New Testament that Messiah, Jesus Christ, was revealed. We read how He accomplished the salvation of humanity from the power and penalty of sin, but we have yet to see the complete fulfillment of all His promises to Israel and all people. This will take place when He returns.

In the meantime, Titus 2:11-14 tells us," For the grace of God has appeared that offers salvation to all people. It teaches us to say 'No' to ungodliness and worldly passions, and to live self-controlled, upright and godly lives in this present age, while we wait for the blessed hope—the appearing of the glory of our great God and Savior, Jesus Christ, who gave himself for us to redeem us from all wickedness and to purify for himself a people that are his very own, eager to do what is good."

---

1. *The Expositors Bible Commentary*, notes on 2 Kings 10:15.

Study Questions

Before you begin your study this week:
- Pray and ask God to speak to you through His Holy Spirit.
- Use only the Bible for your answers.
- Write down your answers and the verses you used.
- Answer the "Challenge" questions if you have the time and want to do them.
- Share your answers to the "Personal" questions with the class only if you want to share them.

First Day: Read the Commentary on 2 Kings 8-10.

1. What meaningful or new thought did you find in the Commentary on 2 Kings 8-10 or from your teacher's lecture?

2. Look for a verse in the lesson to memorize this week. Write it down, carry it with you, or post it in a prominent place. Make a real effort to learn the verse and its "address" (reference of where it is found in the Bible).

Second Day: Read 2 Kings 11-12, concentrating on 11:1-11.

1. When King Ahaziah of Judah, the southern kingdom, died, who took control and what did she do to make sure she stayed in control? (2 Kings 11:1)

2. a. Who took action to thwart Athaliah's plan, and what did she do? (2 Kings 11:2)

   b. Where did she subsequently move the child for long-term concealment? (2 Kings 11:3)

3. a. How are Athaliah and her son Ahaziah characterized in 2 Kings 8:26-27 and 2 Chronicles 24:7?

   b. Challenge: Who was Jehosheba's husband, according to 2 Chronicles 22:11?

4. How did Jehoiada plan to remove Queen Athaliah from the throne of Judah that she had usurped? (2 Kings 11:4-11; summarize briefly)

5. Challenge: Read 2 Chronicles 23:1-2. In addition to securing the support of officials in the military and at the temple, how did Jehoiada make sure the people throughout the kingdom would support the true king? (2 Chronicles 23:1-2a)

6. Personal: The evil Athaliah ruled Judah for seven long years. For those who did not know that the true king was hidden in the temple, it must have seemed that God had forsaken Judah. Yet God's plan—working through the godly princess Jehosheba and her husband Jehoiada the priest—prevailed. Are you facing something today that makes you fear that evil is unstoppable? Do you trust that God's plan will prevail in your life and your circumstances?

Third Day: Review 2 Kings 11-12, concentrating on 11:12-21.

1. How was Joash proclaimed king of Judah? (2 Kings 11:12)

2. How did Athaliah react when she heard the commotion? (2 Kings 11:13-14)

3. What happened to Athaliah because she had usurped the throne? (2 Kings 11:15-16)

4. a. What two covenants did Jehoiada make? (2 Kings 11:17)

    b. How did the people of Judah cleanse the land of ungodliness? (2 Kings 11:18a)

5. What procession took place to finish the day's events, and how did the people respond? (2 Kings 11:18b-21)

6. Personal: Notice that not only did the people return to a covenant relationship with God, but they also renounced and destroyed the center of pagan worship that Athaliah and Ahaziah had promoted. Read Colossians 3:7-12. What is the believer to do when he or she repents and turns to God? Have you done this? Why not pray about this now?

Fourth Day: Review 2 Kings 11-12, concentrating on 12:1-5.

1. a. How long did Joash reign in Jerusalem, and how is his reign evaluated? (2 Kings 12:1-2a)

    b. In what way was this positive evaluation limited? (2 Kings 12:2b)

2. What was a possible source of spiritual problems that Joash allowed to remain in his kingdom?[1] (2 Kings 12:3)

---

1. According to *The NIV Study Bible* note on this verse, "These were high places where the Lord was worshipped rather than pagan deities... They were neverthe-less potential sources for the entrance of pagan practices into Israel's worship."

3. For what reasons did the people bring money to the temple of the Lord? (2 Kings 12:4)

4. Challenge: What do you learn about these three sources in the following verses? (Summarize briefly.)

   Exodus 30:11-16

   Leviticus 27:1-25 (List the things that an Israelite might dedicate to the Lord, for which he may pay an equivalent value in money rather than giving the actual thing to the Lord—see verses 2, 9, 11, 14, and 16.)

   Deuteronomy 16:10

5. What did Joash order to be done with the money collected from the people? (2 Kings 12:5)

6. Personal: In addition to the temple sacrifices specified by the law of Moses, the people brought voluntary offerings to thank the Lord for His blessings. How do you decide what to give to the Lord's work? Do you give "in proportion to the blessings the LORD your God has given you" (Deuteronomy 16:10)? How might your giving change if you did this?

Fifth Day: Review 2 Kings 11-12, concentrating on 12:6-16.

1. In 2 Kings 12:4-5, King Joash had commanded the priests to use the money brought to the temple to make repairs. What was the situation in verse 6?

2. a. How did Joash deal with the situation? (2 Kings 12:7-9)

   b. Challenge: Read the parallel description of this event in 2 Chronicles 24:8-10. How did Joash publicize the need for funds to repair the temple? How did the people respond?

3. How were the collected donations handled? (2 Kings 12:10-15, summarize briefly)

4. Challenge: Second Kings 12:13 specified that the donations from the box were not used for making sacred vessels for the temple as long as repairs to the temple itself were still in process. Read 2 Chronicles 24:13-14a. When the repairs were completed, was there any money left over, and what was it used for?

5. How were the ongoing needs of the priests provided for during the time that monies brought to the temple were being used for repairs? (2 Kings 12:16)

6. Personal: Second Kings 12:15 says, "They did not require an accounting from those to whom they gave the money to pay the workers, because they acted with complete honesty." Do you think the people you come in contact with have this kind of confidence in your character and behavior? Why not ask the Lord to help you be consistently honest and trustworthy?

Sixth Day: Review 2 Kings 11-12, concentrating on 12:17-21.

1. What situation arose in 2 Kings 12:17?

2. a. Read 2 Chronicles 24:15-22, which tells what had been happening in Judah before this threat of attack arose. How did Joash's spiritual direction change after the priest Jehoiada died? (verses 15-18)

   b. How did the Lord, through His servants, warn Joash and the people? (2 Chronicles 24:19-20)

   c. How did the people and King Joash respond to the warnings? (2 Chronicles 24:19b, 21-22)

3. How did Joash convince the king of Aram to withdraw from his attack on Jerusalem? (2 Kings 12:18)

4. a. Read 2 Chronicles 24:23-24. Although the Arameans withdrew from Jerusalem after Joash sent them all the treasure, what did they do not long afterward? (verse 23)

   b. Why were the Arameans able to defeat Judah's much larger army? (2 Chronicles 24:24)

5. There is no evidence that Joash repented. From 2 Kings 12:19-21 and 2 Chronicles 24:25, what happened to him?

6. Personal: King Joash began well, doing "what was right in the eyes of the LORD all the years Jehoiada the priest instructed him" (2 Kings 12:2), but he didn't end well. He listened to godless advisors—"the officials of Judah [who] came and paid homage to the king" (2 Chronicles 24:17)—and let his heart be turned away from the Lord. Are you depending on someone else's faith and example to make you a Christian? If we want to follow God, we must put our faith in Jesus Christ alone. Ask the Lord to help you rely only on Him, and to guide you by His Word and by His Holy Spirit within you.

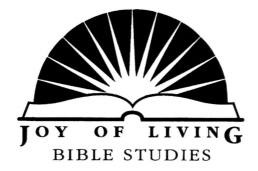

**2 Kings
Lesson 7**

**JOY OF LIVING
BIBLE STUDIES**

2 Kings Chapters 11-12

Setting: The Southern Kingdom of Judah

The writer of 2 Kings now turns back to the southern kingdom of Judah. Chapters 8-9 told of the eight-year reign of King Jehoram of Judah, who "followed the ways of the kings of Israel, as the house of Ahab had done, for he married a daughter of Ahab. He did evil in the eyes of the Lord" (2 Kings 8:18). Jehoram's son, Ahaziah, succeeded him as king of Judah, and ruled for only one year. Like his father, Ahaziah also did evil in the eyes of the Lord. He died of wounds inflicted by Jehu, who also killed Israel's King Joram.

The Reign of Athaliah

When Ahaziah's mother, Athaliah (a daughter of wicked King Ahab of Israel), saw that her son was dead, she decided to take over the throne of Judah herself, and she plotted "to destroy the whole royal family" (2 Kings 11:1). The royal family had already been severely reduced:

🙚 Athaliah's late husband, Jehoram, had killed all his brothers when he came to the throne (2 Chronicles 21:4);

🙚 Jehu had killed another 42 members of Judah's royal family (2 Kings 10:12-14;

🙚 Ahaziah's brothers had been killed by marauding Arabs (2 Chronicles 22:1).

So Athaliah murdered the children of Ahaziah, which were her own grandchildren, along with any others that remained of the royal family.

Athaliah's slaughter was an attempt, by Satan, to completely destroy the line of David. This was an attack on God's plan of redemption. God had promised that the Messiah would come through the line of David (see 2 Samuel 7:11-16), and He would not let His promise fail.

God used a godly woman to fulfill His plan—Jehosheba, the daughter of Ahaziah[1] and the wife of the high priest, Jehoiada, who also served the Lord. Jehosheba hid the baby prince Joash and his

nurse from Athaliah, first in one of the palace bedrooms and later in the temple quarters of the high priest, for six years.

Joash Proclaimed King

When Joash was seven years old, the high priest Jehoiada courageously made plans to remove Athaliah from the throne and to crown Joash as king. He met with military officials and temple personnel, along with the Levites and heads of families from throughout Judah (see 2 Chronicles 23:2), swearing them to loyalty to the true king.

On a set day, the guards that were going off duty from the palace were to come to the temple, where Jehoiada would furnish them with weapons that had formerly belonged to David. These guards were to surround and protect the new king. The guards going on duty were to guard the palace, to ward off any attempt by Athaliah and her supporters to secure the palace for themselves.

When everyone was in place, Jehoiada and his sons led Joash to the appointed place, put a crown on him, presented him with a copy of the covenant, proclaimed him as king, and then anointed him as king. The people gathered in the temple clapped and shouted, "Long live the king!" (2 Kings 11:12). When Athaliah heard the noise, she went to the temple and saw what was happening. She tore her robes and called out, "Treason!" but to no avail. The guards seized her, removed her from the temple grounds, and put her to death.

Jehoiada now led the king and the people in ceremonies of covenant renewal:

🙚 First, the king and the people renewed their covenant with God, that they were His people (see Exodus 19:5-6).

🙚 Second, the people affirmed their support of King Joash as the true heir of the line of David. This covenant "defined responsibilities and mutual obligations of king and people that were compatible with Israel's covenant relationship with the Lord."[2]

Following these covenant vows, the people tore down the temple of Baal, smashing the altars and idols, and killed Baal's priest, Mattan.

Jehoiada led the royal bodyguard in escorting King Joash from the temple to the palace, followed by the military, civil and religious officials and all the joyous people. The king took his place on the throne, and "the city was calm" (2 Kings 11:21).

---

1. It is likely that Jehosheba was the daughter of Jehoram by a wife other than Athaliah, and thus she was a half sister of Ahaziah (*NIV Study Notes* on 2 Kings 11:2).

---

2. *NIV Study Notes* on 2 Kings 11:17.

Not only did the people of Judah return to a covenant relationship with God, but they also renounced and destroyed the center of pagan worship that Athaliah and Ahaziah had promoted. In the same way, when a person repents and turns to God today, we are to "put to death...whatever belongs to [our] earthly nature" (Colossians 3:7). The passage continues, listing some of the things we must rid ourselves of: "sexual immorality, impurity, lust, evil desires...greed... anger, rage, malice, slander, and filthy language...Do not lie to each other" (verses 8-9). The corresponding positive action required is, "As God's chosen people, holy and dearly loved, clothe yourselves with compassion, kindness, humility, gentleness and patience" (verse 12).

Of course, we can't do this by our own power. Only by the power of God's Spirit, whom we receive when we accept Jesus Christ as Savior, can our thoughts and behavior be changed in this way.[1]

Unfortunately, as we will soon see, some of these people did not turn to the Lord with their hearts, but only as an outward show to pacify those who were in power. As soon as they were able, they went back to the ways of the Canaanites.

In times past many people attended church because it was the culturally accepted thing to do. It established a person as an active member of their community. As our society has changed over time, more and more people do not attend church or have any outward show of following Jesus Christ.

Before moving on with this study, why don't you take a moment to search your heart? Have you attended church for the fun and fellowship, or because of some tangible benefit, or have you attended because you love the Lord? What will you do or say if identifying yourself as a follower of Jesus Christ brings you scorn or indifference from the people around you? Do you love Him enough to face persecution for His name? Ask Him to strengthen you and give you boldness to stand for Him, even if others choose not to.

Joash's Reign

Second Kings chapter 12 begins with a positive evaluation of Joash's reign, at least during the time that Jehoiada the priest instructed him—"Joash did what was right in the eyes of the Lord" (verse 1). Unfortunately, "The high places...were not removed; the people continued to offer sacrifices and burn incense there" (verse 3). These were places where the Lord was worshiped rather than pagan gods, but they were not where and how God had instructed His people to worship Him. They may have been potential sources for the entrance of pagan practices into Judah's worship.[2]

Repair of the Temple

Construction of the temple in Jerusalem had been completed 124 years before the beginning of Joash's reign.[3] Its maintenance may have been neglected during the reigns of Athaliah and previous un-

godly rulers in Judah. Joash issued instructions to the priests that the money that was already being brought to the temple was to be used for repairs. There were several sources of funds coming into the temple:

- *The census.* At the age of 20, Israelite youths were required to make an offering of half a shekel (see Exodus 30:11-16).

- *Personal vows.* Leviticus 27:1–25 lists things that an Israelite might dedicate to the Lord, for which he could pay an equivalent value in money rather than giving the actual thing to the Lord.

- *Voluntary offerings.* These were not required by law, but given by willing worshipers. (See Leviticus 22:18-23; Deuteronomy 16:10.)

Not only did Joash give instructions to the priests about the money to be used for the temple repairs, but he also ordered both the priests and the Levites to gather the funds personally from the cities of Judah, and added, "Do it now" (2 Chronicles 24:5). "But," the Chronicler continued, "the Levites did not act at once."

So Joash decided to take action. He ordered that a chest be set at the entrance to the temple, so that people entering might put in their contributions. He also issued a proclamation throughout Judah about the need, urging everyone to participate. Second Chronicles 24:10 reports, "All the officials and all the people brought their contributions gladly, dropping them into the chest until it was full."

Whenever the chest was full, the royal secretary and the high priest counted the money and gave it to those who had been appointed to supervise the work. All funds were initially designated for temple repairs, but when the restoration was completed, additional funds were used for silver and gold articles to be used in the temple service (see 2 Kings 12:10-15; 2 Chronicles 24:13-14). During this time, the priests continued to receive the money from the guilt offerings and sin offerings to provide for their needs.

Judgment from the Lord

In 2 Kings 12:17, the narrative shifts to a later time, perhaps toward the end of Joash's reign.

Hazael, king of Aram (a country located north of the kingdom of Israel), renewed his pressure against Israel and Judah. He marched his army down the Mediterranean coast to Philistia, attacking the city of Gath and capturing it. Then he turned inland to attack Jerusalem.

From 2 Chronicles 24:17-24, we see that Joash had turned away from the Lord after Jehoiada's death. The officials of Judah influenced Joash to follow Canaanite practices. The Lord continually warned them, but they wouldn't listen. They actually stoned Jehoiada's son, Zechariah, for delivering the Lord's pronouncement against them. So when God's patience ran out, He delivered Joash and Judah into the hands of the Arameans.

Second Kings 12:18 says that Joash convinced the king of Aram to withdraw from his attack on Jerusalem by giving him all the sacred objects from the temple and the gold from his palace. But not long afterward, the Aramean army returned. Second Chronicles 24:23-24

---

1. If you would like to learn more about how God empowers and works in us to make us more and more like Himself, you may want to consider doing the Joy of Living Study of Romans when you complete this study.
2. *NIV Study Notes* on 2 Kings 12:3.
3. Ibid, notes on 2 Kings 12:5.

says, "It invaded Judah and Jerusalem and killed all the leaders of the people. They sent all the plunder to their king in Damascus. Although the Aramean army had come with only a few men, the Lord delivered into their hands a much larger army. Because Judah had forsaken the Lord, the God of their ancestors, judgment was executed on Joash."

There is no evidence that Joash repented. Second Kings 12:20 reports, "His officials conspired against him and assassinated him." The Chronicler gives additional details, "When the Arameans withdrew, they left Joash severely wounded. His officials conspired against him for murdering the son of Jehoiada the priest, and they killed him in his bed" (2 Chronicles 24:25).

King Joash began well, doing "what was right in the eyes of the LORD all the years Jehoiada the priest instructed him" (2 Kings 12:2), but he didn't end well. He listened to godless advisors—"the officials of Judah [who] came and paid homage to the king" (2 Chronicles 24:17)—and let his heart be turned away from the Lord.

Joash is a prime example of how we are influenced by others. Whom do you turn to for advice? Sometimes people seek business advice from successful business people that may have greed or worldly success as the driving forces of their lives. Do you believe they would give godly business advice? What about advice on marriage? Parenting? Career choices? Can you see the difference in the type of counsel a godly or ungodly adviser might give?

We are also influenced by what is preached in our church services. Second Timothy 4:3-4 warns us, "For the time will come when people will not put up with sound doctrine. Instead, to suit their own desires, they will gather around them a great number of teachers to say what their itching ears want to hear. They will turn their ears away from the truth and turn aside to myths."

Are you attending a church just because you like the music or because of the activities they offer you or your children? We need to be careful about what is being taught from the pulpit. It will influence the way we think. What we are taught will either encourage us in our walk with the Lord or will focus our trust on something else.

Study Questions

Before you begin your study this week:
- ⮞ Pray and ask God to speak to you through His Holy Spirit.
- ⮞ Use only the Bible for your answers.
- ⮞ Write down your answers and the verses you used.
- ⮞ Answer the "Challenge" questions if you have the time and want to do them.
- ⮞ Share your answers to the "Personal" questions with the class only if you want to share them.

First Day: Read the Commentary on 2 Kings 11-12.

1. What meaningful or new thought did you find in the Commentary on 2 Kings 11-12 or from your teacher's lecture?

2. Look for a verse in the lesson to memorize this week. Write it down, carry it with you, or post it in a prominent place. Make a real effort to learn the verse and its "address" (reference of where it is found in the Bible).

Second Day: Read 2 Kings 13-16, concentrating on chapter 13.

1. a. The chapters we are covering in this lesson describe the reigns of about a dozen kings of both the northern kingdom (Israel) and the southern kingdom (Judah) over a period of about one hundred years. See the chart on page 7, "Rulers of Israel and Judah," to help you navigate this section of Scripture. From 2 Kings 13:1, who became king over Israel, and how long did he reign?

   b. What did this king do that angered the Lord, and what consequences did Israel suffer? (2 Kings 13:2-3,7; review 2 Kings 10:29 to see what this sin was)

2. a. What did Jehoahaz eventually do, and how did the Lord respond? (2 Kings 13:4-5)

   b. When Jehoahaz sought the Lord, the Lord in His covenant mercy sent relief to Israel. However, in what sins did Jehoahaz allow the Israelites to continue? (2 Kings 13:6)

3. a. Who succeeded Jehoahaz as king over Israel, and how long did he reign? (2 Kings 13:9-10)

   b. How was Jehoash's character evaluated? (2 Kings 13:11)

4. a. In 2 Kings 13:14-20a, Jehoash went to visit the dying prophet Elisha. What prophecy from the Lord did Elisha give to Jehoash? Summarize the visit briefly.

b.   God provided another miraculous sign for Jehoash and Israel. What happened in 2 Kings 13:20b-21?

5.   How did God show his faithfulness to Israel in accordance with Elisha's prophecy to Jehoash? (2 Kings 13:22-25)

6.   a.   From Ezekiel 33:11, what do you learn about God's attitude toward the wicked?

b.   Personal: God showed mercy to Israel when King Jehoahaz evidenced the smallest signs of faith in Him (see 2 Kings 13:4-5). Unfortunately, Israel did not truly repent and turn to the Lord, and the next king of Israel, Jehoash, again did evil in the eyes of the Lord (see 2 Kings 13:11). Sometimes when life becomes difficult, people call out to God for help. They really want God's help, but it is just to "fix" the situation—they want to continue living their lives as they please and don't want to truly turn to the Lord wholeheartedly. Are there areas of your life where you merely want God to "fix the problem," but don't want to act in obedience to His Word in order to avoid another such problem? What do you think you should do about this?

Third Day: Review 2 Kings 13-16, concentrating on chapter 14.

1.   a.   Now we turn to the southern kingdom. From 2 Kings 14:1-2, who began to reign in Judah and how long did he reign?

b.   Compare 2 Kings 14:3-4 with the parallel passage in 2 Chronicles 25:2. How was Amaziah's reign evaluated?

2.   a.   What dramatic victory did God give Amaziah? (2 Kings 14:7)

b.   Challenge: Read 2 Chronicles 25:14-16. What sin did Amaziah fall into after this victory, and what would be the consequences?

c.   Challenge: From 2 Kings 14:8-14, summarize how God's judgment against Amaziah came about.

3.   a.   How did Amaziah king of Judah die? (2 Kings 14:17,19)

b.   Read 2 Chronicles 25:27-28. When did this conspiracy against Amaziah begin?

4. a. Returning to the northern kingdom, who was the next king of Israel, and how long did he reign?[1] (2 Kings 14:23)

   b. How was his reign evaluated? (2 Kings 14:24)

   c. What were some of Jeroboam's great accomplishments? (2 Kings 14:25,28)

5. How did God show mercy to His people, even though they and their king were not faithful to Him? (2 Kings 14:26-27)

6. Personal: Both Israel and Judah were experiencing political and economic prosperity during these years, but it seems that God's blessings were taken for granted by their kings. The king of Israel was degenerating into open sin (see 2 Kings 14:24), while the king of Judah did the right things in the eyes of the Lord, "but not wholeheartedly" (2 Chronicles 25:2; see also 2 Kings 14:3). It may take time for the consequences of falling away from the Lord to be felt by a country and in our own lives. Are you enjoying God's blessings? Are you serving Him wholeheartedly?

Fourth Day: Review 2 Kings 13-16, concentrating on 15:1-7.

1. Who was the next ruler over the southern kingdom of Judah, and how long did he reign?[2] (2 Kings 15:1-2)

2. How was his reign evaluated? Read 2 Kings 15:3-4 and 2 Chronicles 26:4-5.

3. What happened to the king? (2 Kings 15:5a)

4. Read 2 Chronicles 26:16-20. Why did this happen?

5. Challenge: Read Exodus 30:7-8 and Numbers 16:1-10, 35. Who was to burn incense before the Lord? What happened to those who were not priests and burned incense before the Lord?

---

1. Note that this was Jeroboam II. An earlier Jeroboam ruled Israel over 100 years earlier (see 1 Kings 12:25ff).
2. Judah's tenth king Azariah ("Yahweh has helped") was also known as Uzziah ("Yahweh is my strength"). Compare 2 Kings 14:21-22 with 2 Chronicles 26:1-2; see also 2 Kings 15:13ff.

6. Personal: King Azariah (Uzziah) experienced great earthly success. In his pride, he disobeyed God's specific instruction in the law, taking upon himself the prerogative of a priest. When Christians today experience earthly success, we can also be tempted to ignore what God has instructed us in His Word. Have you been tempted to do this, or are you facing such a temptation right now? What will you do?

Fifth Day: Review 2 Kings 13-16, concentrating on 15:8-38.

1. a. From this point on in 2 Kings, we will see the northern kingdom begin to decline and eventually fall. Who was the next king of Israel, and how long did he reign? (2 Kings 15:8)

    b. How was his reign evaluated? (2 Kings 15:9)

    c. How did his reign end, and how did this fulfill the word of the Lord? (2 Kings 15:10,12; see also 10:30)

2. Challenge: Second Kings 15:13-31 lists the next kings of Israel after the line of Jehu ended. Summarize each king's reign.

    Shallum (2 Kings 15:13)

    Menahem (2 Kings 15:14,16-20)

    Pekahiah (2 Kings 15:23-24)

    Pekah (2 Kings 15:25,27-29)

    Hoshea (2 Kings 15:30-31)

3. a. The narrator again turns to the southern kingdom. Who was the next king of Judah, and how long did he reign? (2 Kings 15:32-33)

    b. How was his reign characterized? (2 Kings 15:34-35)

    c. Read 2 Chronicles 27:3-6. What were some of this king's other accomplishments, and why was he able to do this?

    d. What happened during his reign that may have been tests of Judah's reliance on the Lord? (2 Kings 15:37)

4. Personal: From the heights of economic and political prosperity, the northern kingdom with its sinful kings had fallen into unrest and trouble. In the southern kingdom political and religious conditions remained stable, but Judah's kings continued to allow the people to continue "their corrupt practices" (2 Chronicles 27:2). From our vantage point it is easy to see the slippery slope they were on, but to the people of that day, it all probably just seemed "normal." Are there "corrupt practices" that the people of our culture, even Christians, take part in today? If God has convicted you of these things, have you repented and asked Him to help you change?

Sixth Day: Review 2 Kings 13-16, concentrating on chapter 16.

1. a. Who was the next king of the southern kingdom, and how long did he reign? (2 Kings 16:1-2a)

    b. How was his reign characterized? (2 Kings 16:2b-4)

2. Who attacked Ahaz, and what was the outcome? (2 Kings 16:5-6)

3. a. Challenge: Read Isaiah 7:1-25. In spite of Ahaz' apostasy, God sent His prophet Isaiah to speak to him. From verses 5-7, who was actually responsible for the defeat of the armies that threatened Judah at this time?

    b. Challenge: The Lord offered to give Ahaz a sign confirming His commitment to the house of David, but Ahaz refused, preferring to rely on his own plans. Nevertheless, God gave him a sign, a prophecy of the Messiah (Isaiah 7:14-15) that would be born of David's line. Although God would preserve the line of David as He had promised, what consequences would Judah eventually suffer because of her apostasy? (Isaiah 7:17-25, summarize briefly)

4. a. Who did Ahaz ask for help, and what did he give him to gain his favor? (2 Kings 16:7-8)

    b. What was the result of Ahaz' request? (2 Kings 16:9)

5. What changes did Ahaz make to the temple worship, either at the Assyrian king's suggestion or to gain his pleasure? (2 Kings 16:10-18, summarize briefly)

6. Personal: Ahaz preferred to follow his own way of dealing with his enemies. It all seemed to go well according to his plan, but God's judgment would eventually catch up with the kingdom of Judah. Do you consult the Lord about your plans? Read Proverbs 19:21; Lamentations 3:37; and James 4:13-15. Why not pray about this?

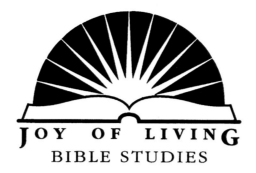

**2 Kings
Lesson 8**

JOY OF LIVING
BIBLE STUDIES

2 Kings Chapters 13-16

Second Kings Chapters 13-16 describe the reigns of about a dozen kings of both the northern kingdom (Israel) and the southern kingdom (Judah) over a period of about one hundred years. It can be very confusing as the narrator switches back and forth between kings and kingdoms. See the chart on page 7, "Rulers of Israel and Judah," to help you navigate this section of Scripture.

Although these passages can seem dry as well as confusing, we receive unexpected benefits from our study of them. We see over and over the fallen condition of humanity—including God's chosen people, the Israelites—but we also see the unstoppable plan of salvation that God is working out through His chosen people.

King Jehoahaz of Israel

Setting: The Northern Kingdom of Israel

Jehoahaz, son of Jehu, became king of Israel in the capital city of Samaria, and ruled for seventeen years. He continued in the sins of his father by following the state religion begun by Jeroboam over 100 years earlier, the worship of the golden calves at Bethel and Dan. Because of this, God allowed Hazael king of Aram to oppress Israel. Due to the Aramean battles, Jehoahaz' army at one point was left with only fifty horses, ten chariots, and 10,000 infantry. In comparison, about fifty years earlier King Ahab of Israel had 2,000 chariots.[1]

At this low point, Jehoahaz "sought the Lord's favor" (2 Kings 13:4). God listened to his prayer and took pity on Israel because of the severe oppression by Aram. In mercy, He provided a deliverer to relieve Israel of Aram's attacks, "so the Israelites lived in their own homes as they had before" (2 Kings 13:5).

Jehoahaz had genuinely sought help from the Lord. He evidently believed that the God of Abraham, Isaac and Jacob could help, however his seeking of help was not true repentance.[2] The worship of the golden calves was allowed to remain active in Israel, and the Asherah pole remained standing in Samaria.[3]

When life becomes difficult, people often call out to God for help. They sincerely want His help, but that is all they want—for God to merely fix the problem, then leave them alone until the next time they need something fixed. God is not an omnipotent genie at our beck and call to fix our problems. He will not accept second place in our lives. As the saying goes, "If He is not Lord of all [in your life], He's not Lord at all."

God, in His mercy, continued to reach out to the people of Israel, but to no avail. They did not understand "that God's kindness is intended to lead you to repentance" (Romans 2:4).

You may wonder why God didn't immediately wipe out Israel for their wickedness. In the same way, as you look around the world and see all the evil that takes place, you may wonder why God doesn't let judgment come now, but the Bible tells us, "Do not forget this one thing, dear friends: With the Lord a day is like a thousand years, and a thousand years are like a day. The Lord is not slow in keeping his promise [of judgment], as some understand slowness. Instead he is patient with you, not wanting anyone to perish, but everyone to come to repentance" (2 Peter 3:8-9).

On those days when you wish that the Lord would "just hurry up and come back," think of those you care about who have not yet accepted the Lord as their Savior, and thank Him for giving them time to repent.

King Jehoash of Israel

Jehoash succeeded his father Jehoahaz as king of Israel, and ruled for sixteen years. His character assessment was, "He did evil in the eyes of the Lord and did not turn away from any of the sins of Jeroboam son of Nebat, which he had caused Israel to commit; he continued in them" (2 Kings 13:11).

An account is given of Jehoash meeting with the prophet Elisha, who was dying. We last heard of Elisha in 2 Kings chapter 9, and there is at least a 43-year period in which we are told nothing of Elisha's activities. Jehoash' words to Elisha, "My father! My father!...The chariots and horsemen of Israel!" (2 Kings 13:14) were similar to Elisha's own exclamation when Elijah was taken up to heaven (see 2 Kings 2:12). It may be that Jehoash recognized that Elisha and the God he served were of great significance for Israel's military success.

---

1. *NIV Study Bible Notes* on 2 Kings 13:7.
2. To repent means "to turn from sin." (Merriam Webster's Online Dictionary)
3. The Asherah pole, a Canaanite idol, had originally been set up by Ahab (see 1 Kings 16:33), and had either escaped destruction by Jehu when he purged Baal worship from Samaria (see 2 Kings 10:27–28) or had been reintroduced during the reign of Jehoahaz. (*NIV Study Bible Notes* on 2 Kings 13:6)

Jehoash had not previously shown faith in God; yet, following Elisha's instructions, Jehoash picked up a bow and arrows, and shot an arrow through the east window. Elisha declared that this was the "Lord's arrow of victory, the arrow of victory over Aram!...You will completely destroy the Arameans at Aphek" (2 Kings 13:17). Upon further instruction to take the arrows and strike the ground, Jehoash struck it three times. Elisha said, "You should have struck the ground five or six times; then you would have defeated Aram and completely destroyed it. But now you will defeat it only three times" (2 Kings 13:19).

The encounter with Jehoash is the last record of Elisha's activities in Israel. Second Kings 13:20 begins, "Elisha died and was buried." However, verses 20b-21 describe one last miracle that took place after his burial, demonstrating the life-giving power of the God he represented. In those days, bands of Moabite raiders would harass the people of Israel every spring. Once, when an Israelite funeral procession was on it way to the burial place, they suddenly saw a group of raiders coming their way. They quickly put the dead man's body in the closest tomb, which happened to be Elisha's. Instantly the dead man was revived and he stood up. What a confirmation, not only of God's power over death, but also that what Elisha had prophesied to Jehoash would certainly come to pass.

In 2 Kings 13:25 we find the account of this fulfillment of the prophecy: "Then Jehoash son of Jehoahaz recaptured from Ben-Hadad son of Hazael the towns he had taken in battle from his father Jehoahaz. Three times Jehoash defeated him, and so he recovered the Israelite towns." God showed mercy to Israel when Jehoash evidenced the smallest signs of faith in Him. His greatness and power were displayed in His answer to Israel's misery.

God is just as concerned about each one of His children today. If we ask Him for help in our own problems, He will give us guidance and help—not based on our great faith, but based on His greatness and power. Have you taken your difficulties to Him, and trusted Him for help?

King Amaziah of Judah

Setting: The Southern Kingdom of Judah

In 2 Kings 14 the narrative turns to the southern kingdom of Judah. Amaziah, son of Joash, was 25 years old when he became king, and he ruled for 29 years. As we will see, however, these 29 years included 24 years in which his son, Azariah, co-reigned, due to Amaziah's foolish actions.

Amaziah "did what was right in the eyes of the Lord, but not as his father David had done" (2 Kings 14:3). Like Joash, he continued to allow sacrifice and offerings in the high places. Second Chronicles 25:2 confirms, "He did what was right in the eyes of the Lord, but not wholeheartedly."

God gave Amaziah a dramatic victory over 10,000 Edomites in the Valley of Salt. Unfortunately, we learn from 2 Chronicles 25:14-16, after the victory Amaziah carried off the idols of Edom, set them up as his own gods, bowed down to them, and burned sacrifices to them.

The Lord, of course, was angry, and He sent a prophet to rebuke him. Amaziah refused to listen, even threatening the prophet with death, so the prophet announced, "I know that God has determined to destroy you, because you have done this and have not listened to my counsel." From that time forward there were those in Jerusalem who began to conspire against Amaziah (see 2 Chronicles 25:27).

Having defeated Edom with ease, Amaziah thought he was invincible. He sent a message to Jehoash, king of Israel, challenging him to battle. Jehoash replied with a parable—Amaziah's challenge to him was like a thistle challenging a cedar tree, only to be crushed by a passing wild animal. Amaziah should be content with his victory over the small nation of Edom, and not challenge a stronger opponent.

However, Amaziah wouldn't listen, so Jehoash attacked and routed the army of Judah, capturing Amaziah in the process. Jehoash went on to Jerusalem and broke down about 600 feet of its walls, carried away all the temple furnishings and palace treasures, and took the hostages back to Samaria. Amaziah probably remained in Samaria until being released to return to Judah after the death of Jehoash.[1]

The people of Judah made Amaziah's son, Azariah, their king when Amaziah was captured and taken to Samaria. Amaziah's return to Judah caused a resurgence of those in Jerusalem who had conspired against him, so he fled to Lachish, a fortress city in southern Judah, but the conspirators sent men after him and killed him there. This was a sad and final end to his apostasy and foolish pride.

King Jeroboam II of Israel

Setting: The Northern Kingdom of Israel

Returning again to the northern kingdom of Israel, 2 Kings 14:23 introduces Jeroboam, son of Jehoash. This was the second Israelite king named Jeroboam. The earlier Jeroboam ruled Israel over 100 years earlier (see 1 Kings 12:25ff). Jeroboam II ruled Israel for 41 years, which included 12 years as co-regent with his father Jehoash and 29 years as sole ruler. Just as his father and grandfather had done, Jeroboam II "did evil in the eyes of the Lord and did not turn away from any of the sins of Jeroboam son of Nebat, which he had caused Israel to commit" (2 Kings 14:24).

In spite of this, Israel prospered both economically and politically under Jeroboam II. He was able to free Israel from the oppression it had suffered from Hazael and Ben-Haddad of Aram, restoring "the boundaries of Israel from Lebo Hamath to the Dead Sea," and extending Israelite political control over the Arameans of Damascus. These things happened "in accordance with the word of the Lord, the God of Israel, spoken through his servant Jonah son of Amittai, the prophet from Gath Hepher" (2 Kings 14:25).[2]

God was faithful in spite of Israel's unfaithfulness. Second Kings 14:26-27 says, "The Lord had seen how bitterly everyone in Israel, whether slave or free, was suffering; there was no one to help them. And since the Lord had not said he would blot out the name of Israel

---

1. *NIV Study Bible Notes* on 2 Kings 14:13.
2. This prophecy by Jonah is not recorded in the book of Jonah in Scripture.

from under heaven, he saved them by the hand of Jeroboam son of Jehoash." But this reprieve would not last forever, as long as Israel's king and people continued to refuse to return to the Lord. God sent the prophets Amos and Hosea to call Israel back to Himself during Jeroboam II's reign; they prophesied against Israel's apostasy, as well as against the social injustice evident among the Israelites. The sin of the Israelites had not yet reached its full measure, and the Lord mercifully extended to the nation an additional period of grace in which there was opportunity to repent.[1]

King Azariah (Uzziah)[2] of Judah

Setting: The Southern Kingdom of Judah

Back in the southern kingdom of Judah, Azariah son of Amaziah became king at the age of sixteen. He ruled Judah for 52 years (10 years while his father Amaziah was a prisoner of Jehoash of Israel, 14 years overlapping with his father's rule after Amaziah had been released and returned to Judah, and 28 years as sole ruler after Amaziah's death).

Second Kings 15:3 says, "He did what was right in the eyes of the Lord, just as his father Amaziah had done," though the high places were not removed. Second Chronicles 26:4-5 adds, "He sought God during the days of Zechariah, who instructed him in the fear of God. As long as he sought the Lord, God gave him success."

Unfortunately, Azariah's success bred pride that led to a severe consequence. Second Kings 15:5 simply states, "The Lord afflicted the king with leprosy until the day he died, and he lived in a separate house." In 2 Chronicles 26:16-20 we learn that after Azariah (Uzziah) became powerful, he tried to take over the priestly privilege of burning incense to the Lord on the altar of incense in the temple. The priests tried to stop him, but he "raged" at them, and immediately "leprosy broke out on his forehead…because the Lord had afflicted him." God had originally instructed Moses in Exodus 30:7-8 that Aaron, the high priest, was to burn incense every morning and evening before the Lord. In the book of Numbers, when 250 Levites and Reubenites claimed that they should have the same standing as Moses and Aaron before the Lord, Moses suggested a test—they would all burn incense before the Lord and see whom He would show as belonging to Him. Numbers 16:35 reports, "And fire came out from the Lord and consumed the 250 men who were offering the incense." In light of this, Azariah's leprosy was a merciful response from the Lord.

Because of Azariah's leprosy, during the final ten years of his rule his son Jotham was made co-ruler to deal with the public. However, Azariah probably retained the true power of the throne during this time.

Decline of the Northern Kingdom

Setting: The Northern Kingdom of Israel

From this point on in 2 Kings, we will see the northern kingdom begin to decline and eventually fall. Second Kings 15:8-31 lists the final six kings of Israel.

King Zechariah of Israel

Zechariah, son of Jeroboam II, became king of Israel in the capital city of Samaria, but he only ruled for six months. He received the same evaluation as his predecessors, "He did evil in the eyes of the Lord" (2 Kings 15:8).

Zechariah was the fourth descendant of Jehu to assume Israel's throne. In 2 Kings 10:30, the Lord told Jehu, "Because you have done well in accomplishing what is right in my eyes and have done to the house of Ahab all I had in mind to do, your descendants will sit on the throne of Israel to the fourth generation." This prophecy was fulfilled by Zechariah's crowning. After only six months, Zechariah was assassinated.

King Shallum of Israel

Shallum son of Jabesh attacked Zechariah in front of the people, assassinated him, and made himself king. He ruled for only one month, when he was assassinated.

King Menahem of Israel

Menahem son of Gadi may have been the military commander of the garrison at Tirzah under King Zechariah.[3] He went to Samaria, assassinated Shallum, and made himself king. He ruled Israel for ten years. He was characterized as doing evil in the eyes of the Lord, just as his predecessors had done.

Menahem savagely attacked the town of Tiphsah because it wouldn't open its gates to him. When Assyria invaded Israel, Menahem levied a tax upon every wealthy person in Israel, in order to give 1,000 talents (about 75,000 pounds[4]) of silver to the king of Assyria. This appeased Assyria, and they withdrew from Israel.

King Pekahiah of Israel

Pekahiah, son of Menahem, assumed the throne of Israel upon his father's death. He ruled for two years, and he did evil in the sight of the Lord.

King Pekah of Israel

Pekah, son of Remaliah, was one of the chief officers to King Pekahiah. He assassinated Pekahiah and assumed the throne, ruling over Israel for twenty years.[5] Pekah also did evil in the eyes of the

---

1. *NIV Study Bible Notes* on 2 Kings 14:27.
2. Judah's tenth king Azariah ("Yahweh has helped") was also known as Uzziah ("Yahweh is my strength"). Compare 2 Kings 14:21-22 with 2 Chronicles 26:1-2; see also 2 Kings 15:13ff.

3. *NIV Study Bible Notes* on 2 Kings 15:14; and *The Expositor's Bible Commentary*, notes on 2 Kings 15:13-15.
4. *The Expositor's Bible Commentary*, notes on 2 Kings 15:16-22.
5. The first twelve years of Pekah's rule were apparently a rival government to that of Menahem established in Transjordanian Gilead. The final eight years of Pekah's rule were over all of Israel after he assassinated Pekahiah. (*NIV Study Bible Notes* on 2 Kings 15:27)

Lord. During his reign, Tiglath-Pileser king of Assyria came and took much territory from Israel, deporting the people to Assyria.

King Hoshea of Israel

The final king of Israel was Hoshea, son of Elah, who assassinated Pekah. He may have been placed on the throne over the remaining territory of Israel by Assyria's king Tiglath-Pileser.[1] The threat of Assyria was postponed, but Israel's end was surely coming. God's prophets, Isaiah and Micah, continued to plead with her to repent, but she would not.

King Jotham of Judah

Setting: The Southern Kingdom of Judah

Back in the southern kingdom, Jotham son of Uzziah (Azariah) came to the throne of Judah at age 25, and ruled for sixteen years. For the first ten years, he co-ruled with his father because of Uzziah's leprosy; for the remaining six years he was sole ruler of Judah. Jotham did what was right in the eyes of the Lord, but, like his father, he left the high places intact.

During his reign, "the Lord began to send Rezin king of Aram and Pekah son of Remaliah against Judah" (2 Kings 15:37). These incursions may have been tests of Judah's reliance on the Lord.

King Ahaz of Judah

Ahaz, son of Jotham, began to rule when he was twenty years old, and he ruled for sixteen years. Unlike his predecessors, "he did not do what was right in the eyes of the Lord his God. He followed the ways of the kings of Israel and even sacrificed his son in the fire, engaging in the detestable practices of the nations the Lord had driven out before the Israelites. He offered sacrifices and burned incense at the high places, on the hilltops and under every spreading tree" (2 Kings 16:2b-4).

Rezin king of Aram and Pekah king of Israel attacked Judah, but Ahaz managed to drive them off. However, they did manage to take some territory from Judah. When they attacked again, threatening Jerusalem, the prophet Isaiah visited Ahaz, assuring him that God had decreed that Aram and Israel would not be able to conquer Judah (see Isaiah 7:5-7). Isaiah went on to prophesy the eventual dire consequences Judah would suffer because of her apostasy. Ahaz asked Tiglath-Pileser, king of Assyria, for help against Aram and Israel, giving him all the silver and gold from the temple and the palace. The Assyrians responded by capturing Damascus, Aram's capital, and killing Rezin. Although Judah was temporarily delivered from her attackers, Assyria herself would eventually become a much worse problem.

As often happens, when we attempt to fix problems ourselves, without looking to the Lord for help and guidance, our "fix" often turns into a greater problem than the original problem. I think of those who "self-medicate" with alcohol or illegal drugs, attempting to cope with the pressures of their lives, when all they are doing is creating even greater problems for themselves and others. Then there are those who borrow money at exorbitant interest rates in order to catch up on their bills, only to find themselves in even greater debt.

Ahaz, indebted to Tiglath-Pileser, went to Damascus to meet the Assyrian king. While there, he saw an altar that impressed him. He sent a sketch and plans to Uriah the priest in Jerusalem. Uriah built the new altar, and when Ahaz returned, he offered sacrifices on it. He rearranged the original temple furnishings and decreed that all future offerings would be made on the new altar, changes made at Tiglath-Pileser's suggestion or to gain his pleasure.

Ahaz preferred to follow his own way of dealing with his enemies. In spite of Isaiah's assurance of the Lord's protection against Aram and Israel, Ahaz turned to Assyria for help. It all seemed to go well according to his plan, but God's judgment would eventually catch up with the kingdom of Judah.

Scripture tells us, "Many are the plans in a person's heart, but it is the Lord's purpose that prevails" (Proverbs 19:21). Do you consult the Lord about your plans? When you face difficulties, do you turn to Him for help, or to earthly sources of help? He is always waiting to hear from you, and He rejoices to work on behalf of His children.

---

1. *NIV Study Bible Notes* on 2 Kings 15:30.

Study Questions

Before you begin your study this week:
- ❧ Pray and ask God to speak to you through His Holy Spirit.
- ❧ Use only the Bible for your answers.
- ❧ Write down your answers and the verses you used.
- ❧ Answer the "Challenge" questions if you have the time and want to do them.
- ❧ Share your answers to the "Personal" questions with the class only if you want to share them.

First Day: Read the Commentary on 2 Kings 13-16.

1. What meaningful or new thought did you find in the Commentary on 2 Kings 13-16 or from your teacher's lecture?

2. Look for a verse in the lesson to memorize this week. Write it down, carry it with you, or post it in a prominent place. Make a real effort to learn the verse and its "address" (reference of where it is found in the Bible).

Second Day: Read 2 Kings 17-19, concentrating on 17:1-23.

1. Who was the next (and final) king of Israel, and what led to his downfall? (2 Kings 17:1-4)

2. a. What happened to the Israelites of the northern kingdom? (2 Kings 17:5-6)

   b. Why had this happened? (2 Kings 17:7-12)

3. How had the Lord warned them? Did they listen? (2 Kings 17:13-17)

4. The northern tribes of Israel led the way in rebellion against the Lord, and were now suffering the final consequences. What was the only tribe not yet removed from God's presence? (2 Kings 17:18)

5. All of this happened because the people refused to honor and trust God, and insisted on being like the surrounding nations. Read 2 Corinthians 6:14-18. How are Christians warned to keep from the same type of sin?

6. Personal: Take an honest look at your own lifestyle. Do you live and act like the unbelievers around you? Is your clothing modest? Do you gossip? Do you grumble and complain? Are you honest in all your dealings? Are you greedy? What do you fill your mind with—on TV, in movies, music, and books, or online? Do you think these affect your relationship with the Lord? Read 1 Corinthians 10:11-13 and Colossians 3:1-3. How can you overcome the temptation to be like those around you?

Third Day: Review 2 Kings 17-19, concentrating on 17:24-41.

1. Who was brought to live in Samaria, the former territory of the northern tribes of Israel? (2 Kings 17:24)

2. When these people were troubled by lions, how did the king of Assyria respond? (2 Kings 17:25-28)

3. Remember, the religion that this priest who had been exiled from Samaria would teach would be the false worship begun by Jeroboam, a mixture of truth corrupted by human additions. In addition to this corrupted worship of the God of Israel, what other religious practices did these people who had settled in Samaria follow? (2 Kings 17:29-34)

4. Challenge: Read John 4:9,19-20. In New Testament times, how did the Jews regard the Samaritans and their religion?

5. Challenge: Read John 4:21-26. How did Jesus say that the religious dispute between the Samaritans and the Jews would be resolved?

6. Personal: No matter what your religious background is, Jesus calls you to faith in Him as the only way to come to God. Read John 14:6. Have you put your faith in Him?

Fourth Day: Review 2 Kings 17-19, concentrating on chapter 18.

1. a. While Hoshea was still king of the northern kingdom of Israel, who became the next king of the southern kingdom of Judah, and how long did he reign? (2 Kings 18:1-2)

   b. How is his reign evaluated, and how was he personally described? (2 Kings 18:3-6)

2. a. Whom did Hezekiah rebel against, and why did he have the confidence to do this? (2 Kings 18:7)

   b. The Philistines were servants of Assyria.[1] What was Hezekiah able to do to them? (2 Kings 18:8)

3. a. Eight years earlier, Hezekiah had witnessed the defeat of the northern kingdom of Israel by the Assyrians. What crisis did his own kingdom now face? (2 Kings 18:13)

   b. How did Hezekiah react to this crisis? (2 Kings 18:14-16)

---

1. *The Expositor's Bible Commentary.* See notes on 2 Kings 18:8.

4. a. Hezekiah's payment didn't pacify the king of Assyria, who sent an army to Jerusalem. What message did he send to Hezekiah in 2 Kings 18:19-25? (Summarize briefly.)

    b. When Hezekiah's delegation asked the field commander to speak Aramaic, the field commander only shouted louder in Hebrew. What did he warn the people of Jerusalem? (2 Kings 18:29-35, summarize briefly)

5. How did the people of Jerusalem and Hezekiah's delegates react? (2 Kings 18:36-37)

6. Personal: We also have an enemy, just like Hezekiah did. Our enemy is the devil, the father of lies. Of him Jesus says, "When he lies, he speaks his native language, for he is a liar and the father of lies" (John 8:44). There is no sense in arguing with him—he's practiced lying to humans since Adam and Eve. It is wise not to engage in a conversation with him; instead think of God and His promises to us. Either read aloud or write out Romans 8:31-39, inserting your name.

Fifth Day: Review 2 Kings 17-19, concentrating on 19:1-13.

1. How did King Hezekiah react to the warnings from Assyria? (2 Kings 19:1-2)

2. What was King Hezekiah's message to the prophet Isaiah? (2 Kings 19:3-4)

3. What message did Isaiah have from the Lord for King Hezekiah? (2 Kings 9:5-7)

4. After hearing the Lord's reassurance, Hezekiah apparently sent a negative reply to the demands of the king of Assyria.[1] Although the Assyrian army withdrew from Jerusalem to fight the advancing Egyptians, what new message did Sennacherib, the king of Assyria, send to Hezekiah? (2 Kings 19:10-13)

---

1. *The Expositor's Bible Commentary*. See notes on 2 Kings 19:5-7.

5. Personal: The Lord told Hezekiah that He would deal with the Assyrian threat, yet Hezekiah had to wait for God to carry out His plan. In the meantime, the king of Assyria was still out there making threats. As believers today, we too face threats from evildoers, and we also can rest in God's promises that He will have the final victory (see Philippians 2:5-11). What threats from evil do you face? Are you able to rest in the Lord as you wait for Him to accomplish His plan?

Sixth Day: Review 2 Kings 17-19, concentrating on 19:14-37.

1. What did Hezekiah do when he received the threatening letter from the king of Assyria? (2 Kings 19:14-19)

2. a. God replied to Hezekiah through the prophet Isaiah. Whom had Sennacherib insulted? (2 Kings 19:22-23a)

   b. After God reviewed Sennacherib's many boasts, who did He say had foreordained these successes? (2 Kings 19:25-26)

   c. How would God deal with Sennacherib's blasphemy and pride? (2 Kings 19:27-28)

3. What sign did God give Hezekiah that He was in control throughout the crisis? (2 Kings 19:29-31)

4. What was God's final message to the king of Assyria? (2 Kings 19:32-34)

5. a. What immediate judgment did the army of Assyria suffer? (2 Kings 19:35)

   b. How was the Lord's word to Hezekiah in 2 Kings 19:7 fulfilled in 2 Kings 19:36-37?

6. Personal: Hezekiah's immediate response to the threatening letter from the king of Assyria was to go to the temple—into God's presence—and lay the matter out before Him in prayer. Is this your first response to a crisis? Or do you try and handle it yourself first? What would you like to do differently?

2 Kings
Lesson 9

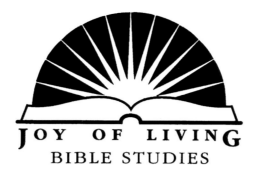

JOY OF LIVING
BIBLE STUDIES

2 Kings Chapters 17-19

As we learned in the last lesson, the final king of the northern kingdom of Israel was Hoshea, son of Elah. Hoshea was a vassal of the king of Assyria, but he decided to try and free Israel from Assyria's yoke. He stopped paying tribute to Assyria, and he sent envoys to the king of Egypt, seeking to join with Egypt in opposing Assyria.

The king of Assyria heard about this, and responded by seizing Hoshea and putting him in prison. Then he invaded Israel and laid siege to the city of Samaria for three years. Finally Samaria fell, and the Israelites were deported to several regions of Assyria.[1] Second Kings 17:7 says, "All this took place because the Israelites had sinned against the Lord their God."

Over 700 years before the deportation, Moses had warned Israel before they entered the Promised Land that this would happen if they turned away from the Lord (see Deuteronomy 28:49-68). Almost 200 years before the fall of Samaria, the prophet Ahijah foretold the deportation to Jeroboam's wife in 1 Kings 14:15-16, "And the Lord will strike Israel, so that it will be like a reed swaying in the water. He will uproot Israel from this good land that he gave to their ancestors and scatter them beyond the Euphrates River, because they aroused the Lord's anger by making Asherah poles. And he will give Israel up because of the sins Jeroboam has committed and has caused Israel to commit." During the final years of the northern kingdom, God's prophets Isaiah and Micah repeatedly pleaded with Israel to repent, but she would not.

God allowed the entire northern kingdom to fall into the hands of the Assyrian invaders. The only Israelite tribe not removed from the Lord's presence was the tribe of Judah, which was in the southern kingdom.[2] Judah had been exempted because she had stayed closer to the true worship of the Lord, though with many failures. It remained to be seen if she would learn from the fate of her sister tribes in the north.

---

1. Assyrian records reveal that the deportations approximated only a limited percentage of the population, usually consisting of noble families. Agricultural workers, no doubt the majority, were deliberately left to care for the crops. (*NIV Study Notes*, "Exile of the Northern Kingdom")
2. The southern kingdom included elements of the tribes of Simeon and Benjamin, but Judah was the only tribe in the south to retain its complete integrity. (*NIV Study Notes* on 2 Kings 17:18).

The Influence of the World

We may look back at Israel and think, "What was wrong with them?! Why didn't they worship only the Lord, who had done so much for them? Why were the gods and practices of the pagan peoples around them so attractive?"

But stop and think about Christians today. God has done so much for every single one of us—sent His Son, Jesus Christ, to pay the price for our sin by dying on the cross; raised Him from death so that we can also receive eternal life; and sent His Spirit to live within us, to guide, teach, and comfort us. Yet, the "world" can be very tempting to believers. We may think that it does no harm to participate in some activities or thought patterns, but they may actually be pulling us away from the Lord, slowly but surely.

If you are a believer, pray and ask God to help you stay close to Him. Pay attention to God's Spirit when He alerts you that something is not good for you to take part in, or that your thoughts and opinions are moving away from His truth. Spend time daily in His Word and in prayer. And remember, "God is faithful; he will not let you be tempted beyond what you can bear. But when you are tempted, he will also provide a way out so that you can endure it" (1 Corinthians 10:13).

New Settlers in Samaria

After the king of Assyria deported the Israelites from their land, he brought people from other areas into the towns of Samaria to replace the Israelites. This was an attempt to make the conquered districts more manageable, by training and encouraging the new citizens to transfer their loyalties to the Assyrian Empire.[3]

God often works through natural occurrences. For example He may send a famine by creating a drought. In this instance, He used the disruption and depopulation caused by the war to cause the population of lions in the territory of Samaria to greatly increase. These lions began to trouble the new residents, even killing some of them. The people of the land viewed this as punishment from the Lord, or from "the god of that country," as a report from the immigrants to the king of Assyria called Him. They were worried because they did "not know what he requires" (2 Kings 17:26).

---

3. *The Expositor's Bible Commentary,* notes on 2 Kings 17:24.

The various people groups had their own gods, and they often believed that a particular god was attached to a certain portion of territory (see 1 Kings 20:23,28). These immigrants did not understand that the God of Israel was the almighty God of creation, the only living and true God, and so they thought to appease Him by acknowledging Him as they would one of their false deities.

So the king of Assyria ordered that one of the priests that had been taken captive from Samaria be sent back to live there and teach the people. The priest that was sent back lived in Bethel and taught them how to worship the Lord. Bethel, however, was the center for the false worship that Jeroboam I had begun back in 1 Kings 12. The resulting religion in post-exilic Samaria was a mixture of God's truth corrupted both by Jeroboam I's additions and by the religions brought by each national group from their homelands.

Nearly 700 years later, in the time of Jesus, the Jews regarded the mixed-ancestry Samaritans with distrust and disdain.[1] They would not associate with them (see John 4:9), and avoided traveling through their territory. By that time, the Samaritans had rejected the idolatry of their past and followed the teachings of Moses, but with a limited understanding of God.[2] They worshipped the Lord "on this mountain" in Samaria (John 4:20), rather than in Jerusalem as the Lord had instructed.

As we can see, although God is patient and longsuffering, judgment is certain for those who stubbornly refuse to turn to the Him in repentance. The northern kingdom was taken into exile, but the southern kingdom of Judah still remained.

God created the Jews (through Abraham, Isaac, and Jacob), to whom He gave His law, and through whom He eventually sent the Savior. In speaking to a Samaritan woman, Jesus said, "Woman… believe me, a time is coming when you will worship the Father neither on this mountain nor in Jerusalem. You Samaritans worship what you do not know; we worship what we do know, for salvation is from the Jews. Yet a time is coming and has now come when the true worshipers will worship the Father in the Spirit and in truth, for they are the kind of worshipers the Father seeks. God is spirit, and his worshipers must worship in the Spirit and in truth" (John 4:21-24).

Acts 17:30-31 tells us, "…now he [God] commands all people everywhere to repent. For he has set a day when he will judge the world with justice." And 2 Corinthians 6:2 says, "I tell you, now is the time of God's favor, now is the day of salvation." Are you still going your way instead of God's way? Are you living as those immigrants to Samaria did, wanting to appease God, but still living as you always have? Tomorrow is not promised to you; today is the "day of salvation."[3]

---

1. These Samaritans had caused much trouble for the Jews who later returned from exile (see Ezra 4 and Nehemiah 4).
2. *NIV Study Notes* on 2 Kings 17:29 and John 4:22.
3. For more information about salvation, turn to page 4, or speak to your Bible study leader, pastor, or other Christian friend.

Hezekiah — Southern Kingdom

Second Kings chapter 18 returns to the southern kingdom, and describes the reign of Hezekiah, who came to the throne at age 25 and ruled Judah for 29 years. Hezekiah received a glowing evaluation: "He did what was right in the eyes of the Lord, just as his father David had done. He…trusted in the Lord, the God of Israel. There was no one like him among all the kings of Judah, either before him or after him. He held fast to the Lord and did not stop following him; he kept the commands the Lord had given Moses" (2 Kings 18:3,5-6).

His father, Ahaz, had led Judah into idol worship, but Hezekiah thoroughly reformed Judah's religious practices, removing the high places, smashing the sacred stones, and cutting down Asherah poles, as well as breaking into pieces Moses' bronze snake, to which the people had begun burning incense. Second Chronicles 29 says that one of Hezekiah's first acts was to reopen and repair the temple, which had been closed by Ahaz. And 2 Chronicles 31:20-21 tells us, "This is what Hezekiah did throughout Judah, doing what was good and right and faithful before the Lord his God. In everything that he undertook in the service of God's temple and in obedience to the law and the commands, he sought his God and worked wholeheartedly. And so he prospered."

Judah had become a vassal of Assyria under Ahaz, but Hezekiah "rebelled against the king of Assyria and did not serve him" (2 Kings 18:7). This means he refused to pay the annual tribute due to the Assyrians. The first part of verse 7 explains why Hezekiah was not afraid to take this drastic step: "And the Lord was with him; he was successful in whatever he undertook." Though refusal to pay tribute would almost certainly bring the wrath of Assyria down upon Judah, Hezekiah depended on the Lord, who "was with him."

The Philistines were also servants of Assyria at this time, but Hezekiah did not fear them, either. He defeated them, "from watchtower to fortified city" (2 Kings 18:8). During his father Ahaz' time, the Philistines had captured cities of Judah in the hill country and Negev (see 2 Chronicles 28:18-19), and Hezekiah was able to reverse the situation.

The Assyrian Invasion

Sennacherib, king of Assyria, did not let Hezekiah's action pass unchallenged. He "attacked all the fortified cities of Judah and captured them" (2 Kings 18:13). Hezekiah sent a letter of submission to Sennacherib, saying that he would pay whatever tribute was demanded. Hezekiah not only paid the 300 talents of silver and 30 talents of gold that Sennacherib indicated, but also emptied the treasuries of the temple and the palace, sending even the gold from the doors and doorposts of the temple.

Hezekiah's payment didn't pacify the king of Assyria, who sent an army to besiege Jerusalem. Sennacherib's supreme commander, his chief officer, and his field commander brought his message to Hezekiah. When they called for the king, Hezekiah sent out his palace administrator, his secretary, and his recorder to meet them. Sennacherib's message was:

• In your rebellion against me, it was a mistake to depend on Egypt, "that splintered reed of a staff, which pierces the hand of anyone who leans on it!" (2 Kings 18:21)

• Depending "on the Lord our God" wouldn't help, either. In fact, said Sennacherib, "The Lord himself told me to march against this country and destroy it" (2 Kings 18:25).

Hezekiah's officials asked Sennacherib's officials to speak Aramaic, so the people of Judah within hearing wouldn't understand, but the commander replied that it was necessary for the people to hear, since they would also suffer the terrible effects of a siege.

Speaking even louder in Hebrew, he urged the people to turn against Hezekiah and surrender to Assyria. Although they would eventually be deported, at least they would still be alive, and would enjoy peace and prosperity. None of the gods of the many leaders that had opposed Sennacherib had been able to deliver their people, so, the commander said, it was foolish for Judah to trust in the Lord for deliverance.

The people of Judah, including the king's officials, remained silent and didn't reply to Sennacherib's officials, as Hezekiah had commanded. But his officials returned to him with torn clothing, indicating great emotion. They reported to the king all that the field commander had said. It must have seemed like the worst situation any of them could have imagined.

God's Response

When Hezekiah heard the report from his officials, he was filled with grief. Employing the traditional symbols of mourning, he tore his clothes and put on sackcloth. Then he went to the temple to be in the presence of the Lord. He also sent a delegation, all wearing sackcloth, to the prophet Isaiah.[1]

Hezekiah's message to Isaiah began, "This day is a day of distress and rebuke and disgrace" (2 Kings 19:3):

• Distress because of the Assyrian threat and what appeared, from a human standpoint, to be a hopeless situation.

• Rebuke because the Lord was even now chastising His people.

• Disgrace because they had challenged the authority of the Assyrians by no longer paying them tribute, and now they realized they did not have the strength in themselves to resist the onslaught of the Assyrians.

Hezekiah hoped that the Lord would rebuke the Assyrians for their ridicule of "the living God," and he asked Isaiah to pray for "the remnant that still survives" (2 Kings 19:4).

Isaiah sent an encouraging message from the Lord to Hezekiah, "Do not be afraid of what you have heard—those words with which the underlings of the king of Assyria have blasphemed me" (2 Kings 19:6).

By God's command, Sennacherib would hear a report that would cause him to return to his own country, and there he would be killed. God would deal decisively with the Assyrian threat. After hearing the Lord's reassurance, Hezekiah apparently sent a negative reply to the demands of the king of Assyria.[2]

Although the Assyrian army withdrew from Jerusalem to fight the advancing Egyptians, Sennacherib sent a new message to Hezekiah, ridiculing his belief in the power of his God to deliver Judah from Assyrian might. Hezekiah, he said, would be destroyed, like the other kings the Assyrians had defeated.

Hezekiah's trust in God continued to be tested by Sennacherib's threatening messages. Would he remain confident that God would carry out His plan?

Hezekiah's Prayer

After reading Sennacherib's threatening letter, Hezekiah took it with him to the temple of the Lord and spread it out before Him. Expressing his faith that God still would act on Judah's behalf as He had promised, Hezekiah poured out his heart to the Lord in prayer.

When he addressed God as "the God of Israel, enthroned between the cherubim" (2 Kings 19:15), he meant that God was the personal God of Israel, who would meet with His people from His dwelling place between the cherubim above the ark of the covenant (see Exodus 25:18; 1 Samuel 4:4). Hezekiah also acknowledged that the Lord is the only true God who controls the destiny of all the nations of the earth.

Sennacherib's ridicule of the living God, classifying Him with all the powerless gods of the countries Assyria had conquered, could not go unpunished, Hezekiah said. He asked the Lord to deliver Judah from Assyria's hand, so that everyone would know that the Lord was the only true God.

Isaiah's Prophecy

God replied to Hezekiah through the prophet Isaiah, first assuring Hezekiah that He had heard his prayer. There were three parts to the poetic prophecy:

A reply to Sennacherib—He had ridiculed and blasphemed the Holy One of Israel, and had boasted of all that he had conquered. But, said the Lord, all Sennacherib's accomplishments happened because the Lord ordained them. Because of his insolence, God would make him return by the way he came.

A sign for Hezekiah—As a sign that God would deal with Sennacherib and deliver His people, Isaiah's prophecy said, even though Jerusalem was now besieged, in what remained of the present year there would be food enough for all from that which had been spilled accidentally in the sowing and had sprung up by itself as an after-growth. For the next year they would again largely depend on grain that came

---

1. This is the first reference to Isaiah in the book of Kings, though he had been active in the reigns of Azariah (Uzziah), Jotham and Ahaz (see Isaiah 1:1).

2. *NIV Study Bible Notes* on 2 Kings 19:5-7.

up of its own accord in random fashion. For the third year, Judah was commanded to resume normal agricultural activities and was assured that they would eat the fruit of their labor.

Included in this sign for Hezekiah was, "Once more a remnant of the kingdom of Judah will take root below and bear fruit above. For out of Jerusalem will come a remnant, and out of Mount Zion a band of survivors. 'The zeal of the Lord Almighty will accomplish this'" (2 Kings 19:30-31). This not only referred to Hezekiah's day, but also to the future remnant that the Messiah would deliver at His coming.[1]

A prophetic declaration—Sennacherib would not even begin the battle of Jerusalem, let alone conquer it. "By the way that he came he will return" (2 Kings 19:33).

Judgment Against Assyria and Her King

That very night, the word of the Lord given through the prophet Isaiah was fulfilled. The angel of the Lord put to death 185,000 of the Assyrian soldiers. When Sennacherib and the other survivors woke the next morning, they found dead bodies everywhere.

So the Assyrians withdrew from the siege of Jerusalem. Sennacherib returned to his capital city, Nineveh, and never again campaigned against Judah.

About twenty years later, two of his own sons assassinated him, fulfilling the Lord's word to Hezekiah in 2 Kings 19:7, "When he hears a certain report, I will make him want to return to his own country, and there I will have him cut down with the sword."

God's Word is sure. Whatever He says, He will accomplish.

Although Hezekiah trusted in the Lord, he was not exempt from trouble and difficulties. And to make matters worse, his enemies attempted to cause both Hezekiah and the people of Jerusalem to doubt that God was on their side. Although we trust in the Lord, we are not exempt from trouble and difficulties. In fact Jesus said, "In this world you will have trouble. But take heart! I have overcome the world" (John 16:33). Although at first it doesn't always appear like it, God is working out our troubles for our benefit (see Romans 8:28-29). Second Corinthians 4:17 tells us, "For our light and momentary troubles are achieving for us an eternal glory that far outweighs them all." God is working from eternity and for eternity. Our difficulties don't seem momentary, but long lasting, and often feel almost unendurable. So what action are we to take? 2 Corinthians 4:18 goes on to say, "So we fix our eyes not on what is seen, but on what is unseen, since what is seen is temporary, but what is unseen is eternal." When we look at our situations from an eternal perspective, we realize they are temporary. And when we understand that the good that God is working in us is also eternal, it changes our view of the situation.

We also have an enemy, just like Hezekiah did. And our enemy is the devil, the father of lies. Of him, Jesus says, "When he lies, he speaks his native language, for he is a liar and the father of lies" (John 8:44-45). He attempts to discourage us with his lies. He also attempts to discourage those around us. He whispers in our mind and through the mouths of those around us. He wants us to believe that God is not good, that He is not concerned, that it is all our fault, that the situation is hopeless, that God is angry with us and won't help, and on and on. It is at those times we have a choice...we either believe God or we don't. Romans 8:31-37 says, "If God is for us, who can be against us? He who did not spare his own Son, but gave him up for us all—how will he not also, along with him, graciously give us all things? Who will bring any charge against those whom God has chosen? It is God who justifies. Who then is the one who condemns? No one. Christ Jesus who died—more than that, who was raised to life—is at the right hand of God and is also interceding for us. Who shall separate us from the love of Christ? Shall trouble or hardship or persecution or famine or nakedness or danger or sword? As it is written: 'For your sake we face death all day long; we are considered as sheep to be slaughtered.' No, in all these things we are more than conquerors through him who loved us." Just think, it is not merely a matter of coming out on top of a situation in this life—we come out far above it all. Remember, God is working His eternal purpose in us, through the situation. He is working to make us like Christ (see Romans 8:28-29).

Are you going through a difficult time? Will you choose to believe God? Why don't you take a moment to reread Romans 8:28-31, right now.

---

1. *NIV Study Bible Notes* on 2 Kings 19:29-31.

Study Questions

Before you begin your study this week:

- ❧ Pray and ask God to speak to you through His Holy Spirit.
- ❧ Use only the Bible for your answers.
- ❧ Write down your answers and the verses you used.
- ❧ Answer the "Challenge" questions if you have the time and want to do them.
- ❧ Share your answers to the "Personal" questions with the class only if you want to share them.

First Day: Read the Commentary on 2 Kings 17-19.

1. What meaningful or new thought did you find in the Commentary on 2 Kings 17-19 or from your teacher's lecture?

2. Look for a verse in the lesson to memorize this week. Write it down, carry it with you, or post it in a prominent place. Make a real effort to learn the verse and its "address" (reference of where it is found in the Bible).

Second Day: Read 2 Kings 20-22, concentrating on chapter 20.

1. a. What message did Isaiah deliver to Hezekiah? (2 Kings 20:1)

   b. What was Hezekiah's response? (2 Kings 20:2-3)

2. a. How did God answer Hezekiah's prayer? (2 Kings 20:4-7)

   b. How did God graciously confirm His word to Hezekiah? (2 Kings 20:8-11)

   c. What do you learn about Hezekiah from 2 Chronicles 32:24-29?

3. a. Who visited Hezekiah, and what did he do for his visitors? (2 Kings 20:12-13)

   b. Challenge: Read 2 Chronicles 32:31. Whom was God allowing to be tested by this visit? What do you think Hezekiah's actions showed?

4. When Isaiah confronted Hezekiah about this visit, what message from the Lord did he deliver? (2 Kings 20:16-18)

5. How did Hezekiah respond? (2 Kings 20:19)

6. Personal: Although Hezekiah had shown a righteous character and devotion to God, his pride at the visit from the king of Babylon's envoys caused him to try to impress them, foolishly showing them all of his wealth. As believers in Christ, although our sins are forgiven, we each still struggle with the sins of our old nature. Do you struggle with pride, or with another sin? Remember, if you sin, God invites you to confess and repent, and He will cleanse and forgive you. Read 1 John 1:9.

Third Day: Review 2 Kings 20-22, concentrating on chapter 21.

1. Who succeeded Hezekiah as king of Judah, and how long did he reign? (2 Kings 21:1)

2. a. Manasseh would have seen God's great deliverance of Jerusalem from the armies of Assyria,[1] yet how is his reign described? (2 Kings 21:2-9, summarize briefly)

   b. Throughout 2 Kings, we see that a godly king would lead the people in righteousness, and then an ungodly king would lead them astray. We can also see this pattern in our present society—there are leaders who encourage people to do right and leaders who, by their actions, make acceptable those things that are wrong in God's eyes. As Christians, the Lord is our shepherd (leader). Read Titus 2:11-14. As we follow Jesus, what type of people should we be, and how should we live?

3. a. What would be the consequences of Manasseh's evil ways for Jerusalem and Judah? (2 Kings 21:10-15)

   b. God gave the Israelites His law when He brought them out of Egypt over 700 years earlier. What warning did He give them in Leviticus 18:24-28? Do you believe God had been patient with them?

4. How is the rule of Manasseh's son Amon described? (2 Kings 21:19-22)

---
1. *The Expositor's Bible Commentary*, notes on 2 Kings 21:1-6.

5. What ended Amon's reign, and what further power struggle took place? (2 Kings 21:23-24)

6. Personal: Under Manasseh and Amon evil again took hold in Judah. Any of the people of Judah who still truly followed the Lord may have been frightened at all that was taking place around them. Evil is still active in our world today. Do you feel frightened by the forces of evil around you? Read John 16:33 and Romans 8:35-39. How do these verses help you?

Fourth Day: Review 2 Kings 20-22, concentrating on 22:1-7.

1. Who was the next king of Judah, and how long did he reign? (2 Kings 22:1)

2. How was his reign characterized? (2 Kings 22:2)

3. Challenge: Read 2 Chronicles 34:3-7. What did Josiah do early in his reign?

4. What major project did Josiah later undertake? (2 Kings 22:3-7)

5. Personal: Josiah became king of Judah at the age of eight, and began to seek God when he was sixteen (see 2 Chronicles 34:3). Then just four years later he began to purge Judah of idolatry, extending his efforts into the territory of Israel as well. After six more years, he began to repair the temple. All of these accomplishments came about because he sought God. Do you ever wonder if God can use you? Have you sought Him, through prayer and reading His Word? When He calls you to do something, will you move out in faith and obey Him?

Fifth Day: Review 2 Kings 20-22, concentrating on 22:8-13.

1. When Shaphan the secretary went to Hilkiah the high priest at the king's request, what did Hilkiah report? (2 Kings 22:8)

2. When Shaphan reported back to the king, what did he do? (2 Kings 22:9-10)

3. How did the king react to what he heard? (2 Kings 22:11)

4. What did he instruct his officials to do? (2 Kings 22:12-13)

5. Personal: The "Book of the Law" that Hilkiah found apparently contained either all five books of the law (Genesis through Deuteronomy), or at least key portions, if not the whole, of Deuteronomy.[1] During this time, believers may have taught one another about God verbally, but the written record of God's law apparently had not been available. What a dramatic effect it had on the king when he heard it read to him! What fear there must have been in his heart when he realized how greatly they had sinned. Look at your own life for a moment. You may have prayed and accepted Jesus as your Savior, but do you believe you are living a life that is pleasing to the Lord? Read Romans 12, then ask the Lord to help you to live a life pleasing to Him.

Sixth Day: Review 2 Kings 20-22, concentrating on 22:14-20.

1. Josiah told his officials, "Go and inquire of the LORD for me and for the people and for all Judah about what is written in this book that has been found" (2 Kings 22:13). How did they carry out the king's command? (2 Kings 22:14)

2. What message did the prophetess have for the people of Judah? (2 Kings 22:15-17)

3. What message did she have specifically for Josiah? (2 Kings 22:18-20)

4. Challenge: Josiah's reforms and godly leadership would not change the eventual consequences that Judah and Jerusalem would suffer, but God promised that because he had humbled himself and responded to God, he would be spared the anguish of seeing God's judgment carried out. Read Jeremiah 17:5-10. How does God know what each person deserves?

5. a. In Old Testament times, trusting in the Lord meant looking forward to the time that the Messiah would come. Today, we know that it is Jesus Christ, the Messiah, who, through His death on the cross, has made provision for our sins to be forgiven. All we have to do is repent of our sin and trust Him as our Savior and Lord. What do you learn from Titus 3:3-8?

    b. Personal: Have you trusted Jesus Christ to be your Savior and to give you eternal life? If not, why not pray about it now? If you would like more information about this, turn to page 4, or talk to your leader, pastor, or another Christian friend.

---

1. NIV Study Bible Notes on 2 Kings 22:8.

2 Kings
Lesson 10

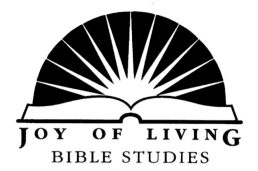

JOY OF LIVING
BIBLE STUDIES

2 Kings Chapters 20-22

Chapter 20 begins with the words, "In those days Hezekiah..." This seems to be a general statement referring to "sometime" in the reign of Hezekiah. The events of chapter 20 probably happened before those recorded in 2 Kings 18:7—19:37, in which the Assyrians carried the northern kingdom of Israel into captivity and then attacked Judah. Although Hezekiah at first tried to placate Assyria by sending all his valuables to them, after Isaiah reassured him of God's support, Hezekiah placed his trust in the Lord. The Lord struck down a large portion of the Assyrian army, and the remaining soldiers returned home to Nineveh with their king. The events of 2 Kings 20, although they are chronologically out of order, are recorded as a striking example of Hezekiah's trust in God.

Hezekiah "became ill and was at the point of death." The prophet Isaiah told him, "This is what the Lord says: Put your house in order, because you are going to die; you will not recover" (2 Kings 20:1). Assuming that Hezekiah was 25 years old when he began his sole reign (see 2 Kings 18:2) and that his illness occurred a little more than 15 years prior to his death (see 2 Kings 20:6), he would have been only 37 or 38 years old at this time, in the prime of his life (see Isaiah 38:9-10).

After Isaiah left, Hezekiah "turned his face to the wall" (2 Kings 20:2) and talked to God. He reminded the Lord that he had faithfully and wholeheartedly followed Him, and he "wept bitterly" (2 Kings 20:3). This was not a prayer asking God's favor because of Hezekiah's good works, but rather was an acknowledgement that the Lord graciously helps those who serve Him.

Before Isaiah had even walked all the way out of the palace, God sent him back to Hezekiah with a message, "I have heard your prayer and seen your tears; I will heal you. On the third day from now you will go up to the temple of the Lord. I will add fifteen years to your life. And I will deliver you and this city from the hand of the king of Assyria. I will defend this city for my sake and for the sake of my servant David" (2 Kings 20:5-6). God is sovereign—He directs all that happens. But that does not mean that we should consider everything that we face to be our "fate." If we are believers, God wants us to bring all of our concerns to Him in prayer. He will lovingly respond to our prayers based on His knowledge of what is best for us within His sovereign plan.

Isaiah not only had a message from the Lord for Hezekiah, he also had directions for treatment of the king's illness. He instructed that a poultice of figs be mixed and applied to Hezekiah's "boil," perhaps an ulcerated sore, and Hezekiah recovered. God chose to work through the medical practices of Hezekiah's day. In our day, He also often chooses to work through available medical services. Ultimately, however, all healing is always from the Lord.

Hezekiah asked Isaiah for a sign confirming all that Isaiah had said. Isaiah offered him a choice: the sun's shadow could go forward ten steps or backward ten steps. Hezekiah chose backward ten steps, a greater sign since it would go against the natural direction of the shadow's movement. Isaiah prayed to the Lord, and the sign was granted.

Hezekiah wrote of this time: "But what can I say? He has spoken to me, and he himself has done this. I will walk humbly all my years because of this anguish of my soul. Lord, by such things people live; and my spirit finds life in them too. You restored me to health and let me live. Surely it was for my benefit that I suffered such anguish" (Isaiah 38:15-17).

Hezekiah's ancestor, King David, wrote of times of affliction: "Before I was afflicted I went astray, but now I obey your word. You are good, and what you do is good; teach me your decrees...It was good for me to be afflicted so that I might learn your decrees...I know, Lord, that your laws are righteous, and that in faithfulness you have afflicted me" (Psalm 119:67-68,71,75).

When we become ill, or are afflicted in some manner, the enemy of our souls—"the accuser of our brothers and sisters, who accuses them before our God day and night" (Revelation 12:10)—often whispers that we have done something wrong, that God is punishing us, or that it has happened and God doesn't notice. However, both David and Hezekiah knew that God was working in them during the time of affliction and difficulty. Hebrews 12:10-11 tells us, "God disciplines us for our good, in order that we may share in his holiness. No discipline seems pleasant at the time, but painful. Later on, however, it produces a harvest of righteousness and peace for those who have been trained by it."

There is no pat answer to the question of why God allows sickness or difficulty in our lives. Each situation is unique, and we must seek the Lord regarding it. We do know that God wants us to ask Him to heal us and deliver us (see Psalm 91:15). We also know that God will use everything—every situation that comes into our lives—and He will use it for our good, to make us more like Himself (see Romans

8:28-29), so that we may bear the fruit of the spirit which is the likeness of Christ (see Galatians 5:22-23).

Hezekiah's Pride

God was not finished doing His work in Hezekiah. Even though God had healed him and given him a miraculous sign, "Hezekiah's heart was proud and he did not respond to the kindness shown him; therefore the Lord's wrath was on him and on Judah and Jerusalem" (2 Chronicles 32:25).

The Apostle John tells us, "Do not love the world or anything in the world. If anyone loves the world, love for the Father is not in them. For everything in the world—the lust of the flesh, the lust of the eyes, and the pride of life—comes not from the Father but from the world. The world and its desires pass away, but whoever does the will of God lives forever" (1 John 2:15-17).

As we can see, pride does not come from God. Just the opposite—all that we have and all that we are is from God, and that eliminates pride and boasting. As it says in 1 Corinthians 4:7, "For who makes you different from anyone else? What do you have that you did not receive? And if you did receive it, why do you boast as though you did not?"

Think about yourself—all that you have, all that you have achieved, and all that you are. Do you sometimes forget that:

- God created you with the talents and abilities that you have?

- God even gave you the drive to achieve what you have?

- God placed you in the life situations that helped shape your character?

- God granted you favor with people?

- God opened doors and made opportunities for you?

The list could go on and on. Won't you take a moment now and join with the psalmist in saying, "Praise the Lord, my soul; all my inmost being, praise his holy name. Praise the Lord, my soul, and forget not all his benefits" (Psalms 103:1-2).

Babylonian Visitors

The king of Babylon, Merodach-Baladan, heard of Hezekiah's illness and miraculous recovery. He sent envoys to Hezekiah with letters and a gift. This was likely not an unselfish best-wishes-carrying delegation, but rather an attempt to find in Hezekiah a new ally in Babylon's struggles against Assyria.

Hezekiah was impressed by his visitors, as Babylon was one of the super-powers of his day. Hezekiah's pride got in his way, and he went way beyond welcoming hospitality. He showed them "all that was in his storehouses—the silver, the gold, the spices and the fine olive oil—his armory and everything found among his treasures. There was nothing in his palace or in all his kingdom that Hezekiah did not show them" (2 Kings 20:13).

The writer of Chronicles tells us that this situation was a test from the Lord—"When envoys were sent by the rulers of Babylon to ask him about the miraculous sign that had occurred in the land, God left him to test him and to know everything that was in his heart" (2 Chronicles 32:31). Although God already knew what was in Hezekiah's heart, his pride was certainly exposed by his actions.

After the Babylonians departed, Isaiah went to Hezekiah and asked him what the envoys had said and where they were from. Hezekiah didn't tell him what they had said, but answered that they came from Babylon. Then Isaiah asked what they had seen in the palace. "Everything," answered Hezekiah.

Isaiah delivered the word of the Lord in response to Hezekiah's pride and foolishness: "The time will surely come when everything in your palace, and all that your predecessors have stored up until this day, will be carried off to Babylon. Nothing will be left, says the Lord. And some of your descendants, your own flesh and blood who will be born to you, will be taken away, and they will become eunuchs in the palace of the king of Babylon" (2 Kings 20:17-18).

After the Babylonian visit, Hezekiah may have hoped that his country would become important as their ally, and that this would ensure Judah's ongoing security. But according to the Lord's word, the opposite would happen—Babylon would invade Judah and carry off its people, even some of Hezekiah's own descendants, along with all its treasures.

At last Hezekiah was beginning to understand, and he replied to Isaiah, "'The word of the Lord you have spoken is good'...For he thought, 'Will there not be peace and security in my lifetime?'" (2 Kings 20:19). His spoken reply appears to indicate humility and genuine godliness, as he realized that his own actions had put his nation and his descendents in danger. The report of his thoughts could be interpreted as a selfish expression of relief that he himself would not experience the coming judgment. However, 2 Chronicles 32:26 reports, "Then Hezekiah repented of the pride of his heart, as did the people of Jerusalem; therefore the Lord's wrath did not come on them during the days of Hezekiah." Hezekiah's thoughts may therefore be seen as gratitude for the intervening time of peace that the Lord in His mercy was granting to His people.

Second Kings 20 closes with a notice of Hezekiah's many achievements. One of these was a water tunnel and reservoir or cistern that greatly reduced Jerusalem's vulnerability to siege by guaranteeing a continuing water supply. Second Chronicles 32:33 adds that Hezekiah was buried with full honors by the citizenry of Jerusalem in the upper section of the tombs of the sons of David.

The Reigns of Manasseh and Amon

Manasseh, son of Hezekiah, became king when he was twelve years old and ruled for 55 years. However, the first twelve years of his rule were as co-regent with his father. His sole reign was for 43 years. By either measurement, his was the longest reign in Judah's history.

Manasseh must have seen God's great deliverance of Jerusalem from the armies of Assyria, yet 2 Kings 21:2 says, "He did evil in the eyes of the Lord, following the detestable practices of the nations the Lord had driven out before the Israelites." After his father's death he descended into terrible spiritual evil, and was perhaps the most wicked of any of the kings of both Israel and Judah. Not only did he rebuild the high places, reinstate the Canaanite worship of Baal and Asherah, and institute worship of the starry hosts, but he even put pagan altars and an Asherah pole in the Jerusalem temple itself, "of which the Lord had said to David and to his son Solomon, 'In this temple and in Jerusalem, which I have chosen out of all the tribes of Israel, I will put my Name forever'" (2 Kings 21:7).

Apparently the people of Judah had only superficially changed their ways when Hezekiah had instituted his reforms. After his death, they quickly returned to evil practices along with their new king. Because of this, the Lord declared through His prophets, "I am going to bring such disaster on Jerusalem and Judah that the ears of everyone who hears of it will tingle…I will wipe out Jerusalem as one wipes a dish, wiping it and turning it upside down. I will forsake the remnant of my inheritance and give them into the hands of enemies. They will be looted and plundered by all their enemies; they have done evil in my eyes and have aroused my anger from the day their ancestors came out of Egypt until this day" (2 Kings 21:12-15).

Manasseh's son Amon became king at the age of 22, and he ruled for only two years. He was as evil as his father. His officials conspired against him and assassinated him in his palace. Then the people of Judah killed the conspirators who had assassinated King Amon. They put his son Josiah on the throne of Judah in his place.

God had given the Israelites His law when they had come out of Egypt over 700 years prior to this. In Leviticus 18:24-28 He had told them very plainly, "'Do not defile yourselves in any of these ways, because this is how the nations that I am going to drive out before you became defiled. Even the land was defiled; so I punished it for its sin, and the land vomited out its inhabitants. But you must keep my decrees and my laws. The native-born and the foreigners residing among you must not do any of these detestable things, for all these things were done by the people who lived in the land before you, and the land became defiled. And if you defile the land, it will vomit you out as it vomited out the nations that were before you.'"

God sent prophet after prophet, warning His people of what would happen if they continued to rebel against righteousness, but as we see, they did not listen. Godly rulers would arise for a time, and those who wanted to worship the Lord were free to do so, but as soon as the godly ruler died, things would go back to they way they were, and wickedness reigned. God was patient, but eventually judgment would come, just as it had fallen on the northern kingdom of Israel.

Whether we are free to worship the Lord or are persecuted for our faith, we should faithfully worship Him, tell others about Him, and serve Him. As the apostles Peter and John said to the rulers of the Jews, "Which is right in God's eyes: to listen to you, or to him? You be the judges!" (Acts 4:19).

King Josiah

Josiah became king at the age of eight. According to 2 Chronicles 34:3-7, in the eighth year of his reign, when he was sixteen, he "began to seek the God of his father David." He began to purge Judah and Jerusalem of high places, Asherah poles, idols, altars of Baal, and incense altars.

Josiah became the last godly king of the Davidic line prior to Judah's exile. The prophet Jeremiah spoke highly of him (see Jeremiah 22:15-16). By the eighteenth year of his reign, when he was 26 years old, he began to repair the temple. When he sent his secretary, Shaphan, to speak to Hilkiah the high priest regarding this project, Hilkiah reported that he had found the Book of the Law in the temple. He gave the book to Shaphan, who read it, first on his own and then in the presence of the king.

When Josiah heard the words of the Book of the Law, he tore his robes. This signified contrition, lamentation, and grief, due to Judah's guilt and her judgment. Under his father Manasseh's rule, Judah had sinned terribly both in their idolatry and in social injustice. Therefore, according to the Book of the Law, judgment must come.

Josiah sent a group of officials, led by Hilkiah, to the prophet Huldah, to ask what the Lord would do regarding Judah's guilt. Huldah confirmed that the sentence of judgment that the king had just heard from God's Word would surely take place. However, because Josiah had responded to God's Word and humbled himself, he would die at peace with God, without having to see the judgment actually carried out.

Josiah's reforms and godly leadership would not change the eventual consequences that Judah and Jerusalem would suffer. But that doesn't mean that they were wasted effort. His own relationship to the Lord, as well as that of the people that sincerely followed him in worship of the true God, was established on the firm foundation of God's Word.

We can have the same attitude and assurance in our day. Although those around us may move into paths that deny God and His truth, it is never a waste of effort to continue to faithfully serve the Lord. We know that the whole world is destined for judgment when Jesus returns in glory (see Matthew 12:36-42; Romans 14:10-12; 2 Corinthians 5:10). No matter what we do, we cannot change that fact. But we can continue to live for Christ and share His message of hope and forgiveness with everyone we meet.

Just as He knows each one of us, God knew Josiah's heart and mind, and He knew what Josiah deserved (see Jeremiah 17:10). Josiah trusted the Lord by following His instructions given in the law, which looked forward to the Messiah that would come to redeem His people. Today, we know that it is Jesus Christ, the Messiah, who, through His death on the cross, has made provision for our sins to be forgiven. All we have to do is repent of our sin and turn to Him as our Savior and Lord. Have you done this? (See page 4 for more information.)

Study Questions

Before you begin your study this week:

- ᴈ♦ Pray and ask God to speak to you through His Holy Spirit.
- ᴈ♦ Use only the Bible for your answers.
- ᴈ♦ Write down your answers and the verses you used.
- ᴈ♦ Answer the "Challenge" questions if you have the time and want to do them.
- ᴈ♦ Share your answers to the "Personal" questions with the class only if you want to share them.

First Day: Read the Commentary on 2 Kings 20-22.

1. What meaningful or new thought did you find in the Commentary on 2 Kings 20-22 or from your teacher's lecture?

2. Look for a verse in the lesson to memorize this week. Write it down, carry it with you, or post it in a prominent place. Make a real effort to learn the verse and its "address" (reference of where it is found in the Bible).

Second Day: Read 2 Kings 23-25, concentrating on 23:1-24.

1. a. The Lord had just spoken to Josiah through the prophetess Hulda. Although God's judgment still stood against Judah for all the evil they had done, yet because Josiah had sought the Lord and humbled himself before Him, God would not bring this judgment about during Josiah's lifetime (see 2 Kings 22:20). Whom did Josiah summon, and what did he share with them? (2 Kings 23:1-2)

    b. What action did Josiah take, and how did the people respond? (2 Kings 23:3)

2. Briefly summarize Josiah's spiritual reforms in Jerusalem and Judah from 2 Kings 23:4-14.

3. a. How did Josiah extend his reforms into the territory that was formerly the northern kingdom of Israel? (2 Kings 23:15-20)

    b. Challenge: Compare 1 Kings 13:1-2 with 2 Kings 23:15-20. How was the word of the Lord given through the unnamed man of God in 1 Kings 13 fulfilled in the 2 Kings passage?

4. In addition to destroying all evidence of pagan worship, what action of godly worship did Josiah order his people to take? (2 Kings 23:21-23)

5. In what additional ways did Josiah carry out the law of God among his people? (2 Kings 23:24)

6. Personal: Josiah zealously purged all evidence of false gods from his kingdom, and led his people in worship of the one true God in celebrating the Passover. Are you as eager to follow God's instructions in your own life? Do you find any evidence of the false religious practices or false gods of our society in your own attitudes, actions, or belongings? Sincerely ask God to show you. If you find them, what will you do about them?

Third Day: Review 2 Kings 23-25, concentrating on 23:25—24:7.

1. a. There comes a point of time when repentance will not deflect God's judgment. God had pronounced judgment on Judah and Jerusalem in 2 Kings 21 and 22:15-17. All that Josiah had done to remove idolatry from Judah merely postponed that judgment. What was God's just judgment against them? (2 Kings 23:25-27)

    b. Challenge: In 2 Kings 22:18-20 we learned that God would spare Josiah from the judgment that was coming by gathering him to his ancestors (i.e., he would die before God's judgment came). What do you learn about this from Isaiah 57:1-2?

2. a. How did Josiah die? (2 Kings 23:29-30a)

    b. What insight into Josiah's actions and subsequent death do you find in 2 Chronicles 35:20-24?

3. a   Who succeeded Josiah as king, and how was his reign evaluated? (2 Kings 23:30b,32)

    b. Who succeeded Jehoahaz as king, and how was his reign evaluated? (2 Kings 23:34a,37)

4. During Jehoiakim's reign, how did the Lord begin to carry out His judgment against Judah? (2 Kings 24:2-4)

5. Challenge: From 2 Kings 23:29,33,35 and 24:1,7, what outside forces affected Judah's rulers? Did Judah's kings consult the Lord as they dealt with these forces?

6. Personal: Throughout history, the nations surrounding Israel and Judah were constantly trying to expand their territory and influence. Some of Judah's kings walked with God and depended on His power, but those that denied God's power had no recourse outside their own strength against these marauding forces. Today, we also face the evil forces of this world. Read 1 Peter 5:8-10. Do you have faith that God will make you "strong, firm and steadfast," in spite of what you may be suffering? Why not pray about this now?

Fourth Day: Review 2 Kings 23-25, concentrating on 24:8-20a.

1. Who was the next king of Israel, and how was his reign evaluated? (2 Kings 24:8-9)

2. Who attacked Jerusalem, and how did the young king respond? (2 Kings 24:10-12a)

3. a. What did the king of Babylon do with the people of Jerusalem? (2 Kings 24:12b,14-16)

    b. What did he do with Judah's treasures? (2 Kings 24:13)

4. Whom did the king of Babylon install as the next king of Judah, and how was his reign evaluated? (2 Kings 24:17-19)

5. a. Why did all these things take place? (2 Kings 24:20a)

    b. Challenge: The prophet Jeremiah served the Lord in Judah at this time. Read Jeremiah 37:1-2. Did the people of Judah repent after experiencing God's judgment at the hands of the Babylonians?

6. Personal: The kings and people of Judah kept making the same choice over and over to turn away from the Lord. Whom do you know who persists in turning away from the Lord? Are you praying regularly that God will change their heart? Perhaps that person is you. Do you make the same choices of disobedience to the Lord over and over? Do you fail to pay attention to the words the Lord has spoken in the Bible? Consider what happened to Israel and Judah. Won't you repent before it is too late? Read 2 Corinthians 6:2.

Fifth Day: Review 2 Kings 23-25, concentrating on 24:20b—25:21.

1. a. What foolish action did Zedekiah take? (2 Kings 24:20b)

    b. What was the result? (2 Kings 25:1-3)

2. What happened to the king of Judah when the Babylonian army finally broke through Jerusalem's walls? (2 Kings 25:4-7)

3. a. What did the Babylonians do to the city of Jerusalem? (2 Kings 25:8-10)

    b. What happened to the people of Judah that had not previously been deported? (2 Kings 25:11-12)

4. What happened to the temple furniture and furnishings? (2 Kings 25:13-17)

5. What happened to the chief religious, military, and government officials of Judah? (2 Kings 25:18-21)

6. Personal: The judgment that God had warned the people about for so many years had finally come to pass, completely and devastatingly. What a shock it must have been to those who had laughed off God's repeated warnings given through His prophets. Is the Lord speaking to you about any area of your life that needs to change? Are you paying serious attention? Why not pray about this now?

Sixth Day: Review 2 Kings 23-25, concentrating on 25:22-30.

1. Whom did the Babylonians appoint to oversee the people left in Judah? (2 Kings 25:22-24)

2. a. What happened to this overseer? (2 Kings 25:25)

    b. What did the refugees who had returned to Judah do when this happened? (2 Kings 25:26)

3. Jehoiachin could be regarded as the last legitimate king of Judah, since he had not been a Babylonian appointee. How did his circumstances change in his later years? (2 Kings 25:27-30)

4. Challenge: Jehoiachin's life can be seen as an illustration of God's gracious concern for His people. Although they had suffered His judgment, He would be with them even during the dark times, and He promised to bring them back home eventually. How does Jeremiah express this in Jeremiah 31:18-23?

5. Personal: The Lord loves every one of His children, even those who have rebelled and gone their own way. He longs for each one to return to Him. He made a way for our sins to be forgiven through the blood of His Son, Jesus Christ, so that there is no barrier to anyone who wants to return to Him. Whom do you know who needs to hear this message? How will you tell them?

2 Kings
Lesson 11

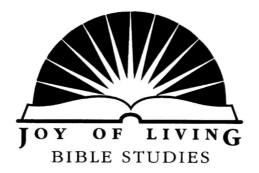

JOY OF LIVING
BIBLE STUDIES

2 Kings Chapters 23-25

Imagine King Josiah's situation. He was crowned king at the age of eight. All around him he would have seen the sinful practices Judah had fallen into under the rule of his father, Manasseh—high places, Asherah poles, idols, altars of Baal, and incense altars. Perhaps due to the influence of his mother and godly counselors, he began to seek the Lord at age sixteen. He started purging Judah of sinful practices, and then, when he was 26, began to repair the temple in Jerusalem. The high priest found the Book of the Law in some out of the way corner of the temple, and sent it to the king.

What a shock it must have been to hear Moses' plain words explaining how Israel was to serve the Lord, and the judgment that would follow if they did not do so. Josiah tore his robes in anguish, then sent a delegation to consult with the prophet Huldah. She confirmed that judgment would certainly fall upon Judah, but because Josiah's heart was responsive and he had humbled himself before the Lord, it would not take place in his lifetime.

So what did Josiah do? He summoned all the elders of Judah and Jerusalem—the leaders of the community due to their position in the tribal and family structure. After that consultation, Josiah called together all the people of Judah, along with the priests and prophets, to come to the temple of the Lord. He read to them the Book of the Covenant that had been found in the temple.

He stood by "the pillar," which was apparently one of the two bronze pillars of the portico of the temple (see 1 Kings 7:15-22), and renewed the covenant "to follow the Lord and keep his commands, statutes and decrees with all his heart and all his soul" (2 Kings 23:3). Then, the narrative continues, "all the people pledged themselves to the covenant." It must have been a very solemn occasion.

Renewed Reforms

Josiah took action to remove all articles of pagan worship from the temple and from Judah. These items were taken outside Jerusalem and burned in the Kidron Valley. Then the ashes were taken to Bethel, which served as a public denunciation of the place where the first official pagan worship—golden calf worship—took place within Israel. He also did away with the idolatrous priests set up by previous rulers Manasseh and Amon, and with male shrine-prostitutes that had served the pagan worship in the temple. He stopped the practice of

child sacrifice to Molek, and pulled down numerous pagan altars, one of which had existed since the time of Solomon.

He even extended his reforms into the territory that had formerly been the northern kingdom of Israel, and was now under Assyria's rule. He removed all the shrines at the high places that the kings of Israel had built in the towns of Samaria, and killed all the false priests that had served at them. He demolished and desecrated the altar at Bethel, fulfilling the word of the Lord to an unnamed prophet (see 1 Kings 13:26-32). It had been about 500 years since that unnamed prophet had pronounced God's judgment on the altar that Jeroboam, son of Nebat, had erected in Bethel, saying, "Altar, altar! This is what the Lord says: 'A son named Josiah will be born to the house of David. On you he will sacrifice the priests of the high places who make offerings here, and human bones will be burned on you'" (1 Kings 13:2).

When God's judgment is not immediate, people often think that there are no consequences for their behavior, that they are "getting away" with whatever wrong they are doing (see Ecclesiastes 8:11). However, God's Word is true and will always come to pass just as He says, in His time. His timetable is not the same as ours. Second Peter 3:8-9 tells us, "But do not forget this one thing, dear friends: With the Lord a day is like a thousand years, and a thousand years are like a day. The Lord is not slow in keeping his promise, as some understand slowness. Instead he is patient with you, not wanting anyone to perish, but everyone to come to repentance."

This study in Kings has reminded us again and again that God is patient and forgiving. However, His judgment is real and will eventually be carried out. It reminds us that we are responsible for what we do, and for what we leave undone (see James 4:17). Hebrews 4:13 warns us, "Nothing in all creation is hidden from God's sight. Everything is uncovered and laid bare before the eyes of him to whom we must give account." There is forgiveness in Jesus Christ, but we must accept it (see John 1:12, Acts 10:43). Then when we do, we are forgiven, but God will discipline us when we, His children, live in rebellion towards Him by not repenting and asking for forgiveness (see 1 Corinthians 11:32). This study also repeatedly reminds us that we need to warn others, while there is still time (see 2 Corinthians 6:2).

Josiah's reforms weren't all negative and destructive. He instituted godly worship among the people of Judah by ordering them to celebrate the Passover according to the instructions given in the Book of the Covenant. Scripture says, "Neither in the days of the judges who led Israel nor in the days of the kings of Israel and the kings of Judah had any such Passover been observed" (2 Kings 23:22). How amazing it must have been, especially as it probably hadn't been observed at all during the many years after the death of King Hezekiah.

As Christians today, we do not have ceremonial law to follow. However, the Lord does command us to separate ourselves from idolatry, to "come out from them and be separate" (2 Corinthians 6:17). What kinds of idolatry do you see taking place in your culture and community? It may not be people bowing down to a statue of a god. But there are certainly many things other than the Lord that people hold as the most important thing in their lives, things in which they find their security. If you identify any of this type of "idol" in your own life, what will you do to remove it? How will you turn to the Lord to truly worship Him, holding him in the highest place of honor in your life, and finding your security and hope in Him? Why not pray about this now?

The End of Josiah's Reign

Second Kings 23:29 says, "Pharaoh Necho king of Egypt went up to the Euphrates River to help the king of Assyria." Egypt was allied with Assyria against the rising power of Babylon. Josiah may have feared that the growth of either Egyptian or Assyrian power would threaten Judah's independence, so he marched out to meet the Egyptians in battle, trying to hinder their route to join the Assyrians. Second Chronicles says that at God's command, Necho sent messengers to Josiah, trying to prevent the battle: "It is not you I am attacking at this time, but the house with which I am at war. God has told me to hurry; so stop opposing God, who is with me, or he will destroy you" (2 Chronicles 35:21). Josiah, however, would not turn back. He disguised himself and went into the fight. Archers shot and wounded him, and he was taken back to Jerusalem, where he died. His actions had brought about his tragic death, but he was spared the greater tragedy of seeing the death of Judah only 23 years later.

Josiah received a ringing commendation: "Neither before nor after Josiah was there a king like him who turned to the Lord as he did—with all his heart and with all his soul and with all his strength, in accordance with all the Law of Moses" (2 Kings 23:25). However, although Josiah's repentance and reforms postponed God's judgment for a time, it would still come to pass.

Despite all that Josiah had done, the effects of Manasseh's terrible wickedness had a permanent effect on Judah. Although Judah's ceremonial worship had been restored in accordance with the law, the people's pledge to renew the covenant must have been just an external change, without a true change of heart. After Josiah died, they again turned away from the Lord (see Jeremiah 5).

Babylon Attacks

The people of Judah named Josiah's son Jehoahaz as king. He did not follow in his father's footsteps—"He did evil in the eyes of the Lord, just as his predecessors had done" (2 Kings 23:32). Within three months, Pharaoh Necho replaced Jehoahaz as king of Judah with Josiah's son Eliakim, changing his name to Jehoiakim. Jehoiakim also

"did evil in the eyes of the Lord" (2 Kings 23:37). Pharaoh Necho took Jehoahaz as a captive to Egypt, where he remained until his death. Judah then had to pay tribute to Pharaoh Necho.

Nebuchadnezzar king of Babylon defeated Egypt and Jehoiakim became his vassal. After three years, seeing that Egypt's strength had returned, Jehoiakim rebelled against Babylon. Nebuchadnezzar was rebuilding his armed forces and couldn't yet deal with Judah directly. However, under the Lord's plan of judgment, Babylonian, Aramean, Moabite, and Ammonite raiders began to attack Judah.

Nebuchadnezzar of Babylon finally set out with his vast army to confront the rebellious Jehoiakim. However, before the Babylonians arrived Jehoiakim died, and his son Jehoiachin succeeded him as king. When Babylon laid siege to Jerusalem three months later, Jehoiachin, his family, and his officials surrendered. Everyone except the poorest people of Judah was taken into exile to Babylon. Nebuchadnezzar took all the remaining treasures from the temple of the Lord and from the royal palace.

After installing Josiah's remaining son, Mattaniah, renamed Zedekiah, on the throne of Judah, Nebuchadnezzar left the city of Jerusalem standing and returned to Babylon. Zedekiah ruled for eleven years, and he also did evil in the eyes of the Lord. Jeremiah 37:2 says Zedekiah and the remaining people of Judah did not repent: "Neither he nor his attendants nor the people of the land paid any attention to the words the Lord had spoken through Jeremiah the prophet."

The Final Judgment

Zedekiah had sworn allegiance to Nebuchadnezzar (see Ezekiel 17:13), had sent envoys to Babylon (see Jeremiah 29:3), and had made a personal visit (see Jeremiah 51:59). Foolishly, he now rebelled against Babylon, hoping to gain independence for Judah.

Nebuchadnezzar returned to Jerusalem with his army and laid siege. After months of waiting, when there was severe famine in the city, the Babylonians broke through the city walls. Zedekiah fled, but the Babylonians captured him and brought him before Nebuchadnezzar. His sons were killed before his eyes, and then they put out his eyes, bound him with bronze shackles, and took him to Babylon.

The Babylonians burned and broke down all of Jerusalem, including the temple and the royal palace. Most of the remaining people were carried off into exile, though some of the poorest were left in Judah to work in the vineyards and fields. Everything that had been made of precious metals was taken from the temple, including all the bronze articles used in the temple service and all the decorations. All the chief religious, military, and government officials were executed.

The judgment that God had warned the people about for so many years had finally come to pass, completely and devastatingly.

Judah in Exile

Nebuchadnezzar appointed Gedaliah to govern the people he left behind in Judah. Many surviving soldiers of Judah who had fled made their way back to Jerusalem to lay down their arms and return to civilian life. Gedaliah encouraged them to settle down and serve the king of Babylon. Unfortunately, Gedaliah was assassinated. The refugees who had returned to Judah were afraid the Babylonians would blame them, so they all fled to Egypt.

Years later, after Jehoiachin, the last legitimate king of Judah, had been in Babylonian exile for 37 years, Nebuchadnezzar died and his son Awel-Marduk succeeded him as king of Babylon. Jehoiachin was released from prison, given a seat of honor at the king's table in Babylon, and given a regular allowance for the rest of his life.

On this hopeful note the book of Kings ends. The judgment of exile would not destroy the people of Israel or the house of David. God would be with them through the dark times, and He promised eventually to bring them back home: "This is what the Lord Almighty, the God of Israel, says: 'When I bring them back from captivity, the people in the land of Judah and in its towns will once again use these words: "The Lord bless you, you prosperous city, you sacred mountain" ' " (Jeremiah 31:23)

The books of Ezra and Nehemiah describe the return of the people of Judah from Babylon to their own land, many years later. And the gospels of the New Testament tell of the advent of Jesus Christ, born of the line of David, in fulfillment of God's promise to His people. God's plan will not fail—His purposes will be accomplished.

This is the end of the study on 2 Kings. There are no questions for Lesson 11.

Notes

Notes

Notes

Notes

Notes

Notes

Notes